Self-Injury:

A Manual for School Professionals

S.A.F.E. ALTERNATIVES®
Self Abuse Finally Ends

selfinjury.com
800-DONTCUT®
(800-366-8288)

Cover design by Mercury & Sun Marketing and Design

Virgin Ink Press

Printed in Chicago, IL

Self-Injury:

A Manual for School Professionals

S.A.F.E. ALTERNATIVES®

NOTE: Look for the *Student Workbook* published by Virgin Ink Press that coordinates with this manual for professionals.

VirginInkPress.com

800-366-8288

ISBN: 978-1-933930-06-0

ISBN: 1-933930-06-3

TABLE OF CONTENTS

Section IV: Instructions for Using Student Workbook

Section V: Workbook Exercises

Section I

INTRODUCTION

BEGINNINGS

Since writing our book *Bodily Harm: the Breakthrough Healing Program for Self-Injurers*, we have received numerous requests from a variety of school professionals asking us to publish a manual addressing ways to respond to the growing phenomenon of self-harm in schools. Self-injury, once an obscure psychiatric symptom, is now a mainstream problem. Therefore, it is imperative that school professionals be prepared to identify, understand and assess students who may be engaging in self-injurious behaviors. In an effort to respond to this need, we at S.A.F.E. ALTERNATIVES® have developed a comprehensive program and manual designed to aid professionals in these endeavors. In addition, we recognize the unique role that each profession brings to the process and therefore have included sections for teachers, nurses and mental health professionals (i.e., counselors, social workers, psychologists).

Self-injurers have historically considered their self-injury to be a shameful secret. However, some students are beginning to glorify the behavior. We view this as a rationalization and it does not change the emotional pain that self-injury represents. Many counselors believe that self-injurious behavior connotes a dangerous and difficult student. While this can be true, recognizing self-injury as an effort to maintain emotional equilibrium can help a counselor maintain empathy by bringing the behavior into a more familiar frame of reference. It is our experience that with the proper tools, as well as an understanding of student and counselor limitations, the therapeutic relationship can be rewarding and productive.

School professionals are often the first adults to learn of a student's self-injurious behavior. It is therefore imperative that all personnel who work directly with students feel comfortable and confident to intervene should this behavior come to their attention. We hope that this manual will supplement the protocol already in place at your school and increase awareness and insight into these behaviors. By providing assessment and intervention tools and techniques that we have developed and determined to be highly effective, we are confident that schools will be able to help save many students from suffering needlessly.

After reading this manual you will be able to:

- Define self-injury

- Identify the various forms of self-injury

- Recognize the physical and emotional signs of self-injury

- Understand the multi-tiered purposes of self-injury

- Help students identify and label emotions

- Help students explore issues that may underlie intense emotional states

- Have tools necessary to intervene with self-injuring students

- Identify resources and treatment available for self-injury

- Learn how to talk to parents about self-injury

Section II

SELF-INJURY

WHAT?   UNDERSTANDING THE BEHAVIOR

Self-injury is basically defined as deliberate self-inflicted harm resulting in tissue damage without the conscious intent of suicide. Behaviors include but are not limited to cutting, burning, head banging, interfering with the healing of wounds, hitting or biting oneself. Unlike most addictions or addictive-like behaviors, self-injury is not a behavior to which a healthy person can relate. For example, many of us have had the experience of consuming one too many drinks and regretting it the next morning, or savoring a great meal while simultaneously planning a new diet. We can, therefore, understand how someone might develop an eating disorder or lose oneself to alcohol. Perhaps due to this capacity to relate, parents and school officials seem increasingly willing to admit to and address substance abuse and eating disorders. Self-injury, on the other hand, continues to frighten and even repulse many people, including the very professionals into whose care these students are entrusted.

Self-injury is a counter-intuitive behavior. That is, survival is a biological imperative; we inherently avoid pain and injury in an effort to survive. The idea that someone would purposely hurt themselves (an act that to some flies in the face of reason) is therefore frightening. That which we fear often becomes the object of our anger.

Attitudes about the ability to overcome pain can be paradoxical. For example, athletes are revered when they play despite injuries. Let's not forget the world wide attention given to the hiker who chose to cut off his arm when it became trapped in a boulder in order to save his life. We were mesmerized by the story, each of us wondering what we would have done in a similar situation. Self-injurers are attempting to free themselves as well, but in their case it is freedom from the weight of intense emotional states which they fear they cannot survive. In other words, just like the hiker, their act of injuring is an act of self-preservation, not an act of self-destruction.

Despite the increase in self-injury among adolescents, there is still a stigma attached to the behavior. Unlike the use of substances or the abuse of food, there is no safe amount of self-injury. In addition, this is not a behavior that works for someone who is not in acute emotional distress. A healthy person who takes a razor to herself to better understand what all the fuss is about is not likely to try it again. It is important for care-givers to recognize that self-injury, like substance abuse and eating disorders, is a coping strategy used by people who are in emotional distress. In short, we at S.A.F.E. ALTERNATIVES® view self-injury as a behavior and not a disease. Self-injury is not a meaningless habit, but rather a behavior that can serve a number of purposes and hold a myriad of meanings. It can at once soothe, punish, numb, repulse and cleanse. It can represent an expression of anger, loneliness, invisibility, fear, self-loathing and even strength.

The philosophy of the S.A.F.E.ALTERNATIVES® Program is that self-injury, while acknowledged as a coping strategy, is considered to be unhealthy. Left unaddressed, it can potentially interfere with all aspects of a person's life. Self-injurers often believe that their behavior only hurts themselves and that they should have the right to treat their bodies in any way they choose. Some believe that self-injury is the only coping strategy that will work for them, and that without it, they could die. It is often necessary for these students to understand their fears, as well as their own denial system, before they can actively engage in the treatment process. It is therefore imperative that professionals who interface with these students be able to understand and address these issues so that students can move past fear and embrace alternative possibilities.

Another important step for self-injurers is to become cognizant of their urges to injure and realize that the urge is no more than a clue that they want to rid themselves of an uncomfortable feeling state. They might be overwhelmed with intense feelings such as anger, sadness and fear; or conversely, they might be so numbed that they are not feeling anything. In the latter, seeing the blood or experiencing any sense of pain serves to reassure them that they are, in fact, alive.

With the help of therapy, self-injurers hopefully will begin to understand that while their injuries can indeed place them in physical danger; it is the inability to identify, feel and articulate one's emotional states that puts them at true risk. Being able to recognize, express and accept the full range of emotions is paramount if the adolescent is ever going to feel comfortable in his or her own skin. A necessary goal of any intervention is to help the adolescent get past the mask that he or she often shows to the world, and allow others to see his or her genuine feelings.

Self-injuring adolescents also need help in learning to differentiate a thought from a feeling and/or a behavior. The English language is replete with examples of how we interchange the two. For example, one might say, I feel like dancing. However, dancing is a behavior and not a feeling. Similarly, self-injurers might often state that they feel like self-injuring, but like dancing, self-injury is not a feeling. It is important for self-injurers to know what they are *feeling* rather than what they are thinking or what they want to do in response to that feeling. Paying attention to semantics may seem irrelevant, but our goal is to help students identify their feelings as separate from their thoughts and actions; using language accurately can help towards this end.

Adolescents are encouraged to challenge the irrational thoughts which serve to fuel intense emotional states. Examples of catastrophic and dichotomous thoughts might include: nothing will ever change, or nobody understands my pain and I have to injure to make them understand. Such thinking styles, combined with a chronically low self image, tend to increase their sense of anxiety, fear, anger and/or depression, making it more likely for sufferers to reach for the quick fix of self-harm.

Being in control is frequently a central issue for those who self-injure. The act of self-injury is, in itself, most often an attempt to stay in control of one's emotions which are often experienced as spiraling out of control and dangerous. They attempt to remain in control by divesting themselves of uncomfortable emotions. Self-injury does generally work towards this end, creating a quick and effective sense of calm. Although those that self-injure might feel better temporarily, they are not better. They have only served to put a band-aid on a festering wound. Without identifying and dealing with the source of the emotional upheaval, the emotional roller coaster is doomed to repeat itself over and over again.

WHY?   PURPOSES OF SELF-INJURY

Self-injury is a complicated set of behaviors that serve a myriad of purposes. Each individual who self-injures may do so due to one, or more likely, a combination of the following reasons. The student may or may not be fully aware of the reasons they injure. Understanding one's motivation is generally a goal of treatment.

Analgesic or palliative aims

Included in this category is the physical calming that most people experience when they self-injure. The self-injurer generally experiences emotional pain and distress as overwhelming. Anxious feelings can quickly turn into severe anxiety or a panic attack. After harming him/herself, an immediate sense of calm generally ensues. One biological hypothesis suggests that when the self-injurer is in an acute state of emotional distress and responds by harming herself, the brain reacts to this pain and stress by releasing naturally occurring chemicals (endorphins) that serve to both reduce feelings of pain and lessen the negative effects of stress.

Connecting body and mind

For students who feel distanced from reality, isolated or dehumanized, the sight of their own blood may jolt them back from a state of numbness to the reality of being alive. For students who feel extremely overwhelmed or anxious, self-injury may provide a calming effect. Although it may sound contradictory, self-injury does seem to serve both poles of feeling: those who feel too much, as well as those who are numbed and feel too little.

Control

One of the most common functions of the self-injurious act is to control one's emotional life by ridding oneself of uncomfortable and unwanted feeling states. Those who have been physically or sexually abused may reenact the abuse in an effort to master control over their body. Many state that they want to master the pain, so that no one can ever hurt them again.

Cleansing

Most of us are familiar with the term bad blood as well as the medical practice of blood-letting which is performed in an attempt to cure people who are ill. The problem is that the blood is not the cause of the dis-ease. In the case of self-injurers, blood is the symbol for toxic feelings which are what the person is actually trying to purge.

Punishment

Students may say they are trying to atone for being inherently sinful or for past transgressions. However, when asked what terrible things they have done, they are frequently at a loss for words. Even if they have engaged in behaviors for which they are ashamed, the punishment they inflict on themselves almost always far exceeds any crime they may have committed.

Words cannot express my pain

Most self-injurers state that they felt neglected, unheard and misunderstood while growing up. They say that their harmful acts show how much pain they are suffering, in a way that language cannot.

Combating a sense of invisibility

Self-injurers report a variety of strong, visceral reactions from others, ranging from deep concern and sympathy to utter revulsion and disdain. Self-injurers report that it is most disturbing when others show no reaction, as this serves to confirm their worst fear, that they are indeed invisible.

The rescue fantasy

Self-injury often represents a desperate attempt to engage people's caring responses. The fantasy is that if people really cared enough they would keep her from self-injuring. The student ultimately finds that her strategies are counterproductive in that self-inflicted violence serves to frighten and alienate others rather than bring them closer. Issues with interpersonal boundary serve to exacerbate already strained relationships. Self-injury begins to replace relationships that are lost.

Vengeance

Many self-injurers fantasize about vengeance on people who have caused them pain. Since sufferers are frequently unable to put their feelings into words, self-injury becomes an outlet for feelings of hurt and anger.

WHEN? WHY NOW?

Parts of this section were taken from an article entitled "A Look at Body Focused Behavior", written by Wendy Lader, Ph.D., co-founder and Clinical Director of S.A.F.E. ALTERNATIVES®, Vol. 11(1) & Vol. 9(4) (Winter 2006) — Reprinted with permission of *Paradigm* magazine, Frisco, TX (214-295-6332).

Wherever one looks today, it is difficult to escape the increasing focus on the body. We starve it, exercise it, tattoo it, pierce it, self-mutilate and modify it through plastic surgery.

For the past 20 years, we at S.A.F.E. ALTERNATIVES® have focused on understanding and treating those who physically injure themselves. We view self-injury not as a meaningless habit, but rather a behavior that can serve a number of purposes and hold a myriad of different meanings. Why is self-injury, which was once considered to be an obscure psychiatric symptom, now seeping into the mainstream and fabric of our society? Should we just accept self-injury as another cultural fad, or is there a deeper meaning to the choice of this particular set of behaviors? Is it purely coincidental that people in our society are turning to more permanent avenues of self-expression with their bodies serving as the canvas? In other words, why are people now experiencing a need to display their innermost thoughts and feelings on their bodies?

The body represents the individual to the outside world; this is how we are recognized from one another. The skin serves as the boundary between "me" and "other". For centuries, and in a variety of cultures, the skin has been utilized as a parchment on which to communicate any number of messages. It therefore makes sense that the body can represent a personal bulletin board to express to others things about oneself.

As mental health professionals we frequently consider and ask the question, "Why now?" At S.A.F.E. we believe that we are seeing an increase in body-focused behaviors for a myriad of cultural reasons and that they are not merely a pointless fad. We live in a society that is becoming increasingly disenfranchised. Following are some of the major changes that have occurred in our society which might contribute to a sense of "invisibility" and alienation in our teens.

Divorce

Increase in the divorce rate necessitating that kids live in two different homes, often only seeing one of their parents infrequently and sometimes never again. Even if both parents remain in their lives, they often have to negotiate the tenuous relationships that accompany parents' dates or "blended" families.

Transient lives

Corporate changes and divorce often necessitate a physical move, sometimes across the county or even the world. This brings about the loss of extended family and friends. We no longer have a "village" raising our children, nor do adults have the support that closer communities used to provide.

Stranger danger

Our society has become more dangerous and younger people have been indoctrinated with the "stranger danger" philosophy of safety. They are taught to not make eye contact or speak with strangers. They can no longer ride their bikes or walk to school alone. Is it any wonder that our youth often experience themselves as alienated and alone?

Technology

There was a time not so long ago when neighbors sat out on their front porches and knew each other well. They played cards and board games with live people. Now adolescents and teens spend much of their time online, chatting or playing games with faceless strangers. Even when outside, amongst other people, they are frequently so absorbed with listening to their iPods or talking on their cell phones, that they barely notice, much less acknowledge, someone right in front of them.

FACTS ABOUT SELF-INJURY

Definition

Self-injury is also termed *self-mutilation, self-harm, self-abuse, non-suicidal self-injury (NSSI) or cutting.* The behavior is defined as the deliberate, repetitive, impulsive, non-lethal harming of one's self. Self-injury includes but is not limited to: 1) cutting; 2) scratching; 3) picking scabs or interfering with wound healing; 4) burning; 5) punching self or objects; 6) infecting oneself; 7) inserting objects in skin; 8) bruising or breaking bones; and 9) some forms of hair-pulling. These behaviors, which pose serious risks, may be symptoms of a mental health problem that can be treated.

Incidence and onset

Experts estimate the incidence of at least occasional self-injury in the general population is nearly 4%, with an almost equal number of males and females, although more females present for treatment. Recent studies of high school and college students put the number at approximately one in five. The typical onset of self-harming acts is at puberty, although it can be seen in young children as well as adults. The behaviors often last for 5-10 years, but can persist much longer without appropriate treatment.

Background of self-injurers

Self-injury is found in almost equal numbers in all ethnic groups. Nearly 50% report physical and/or sexual abuse during their childhood, but it is important to note that it also means that at least 50% do not have histories of physical or sexual abuse. Many report that they were discouraged from expressing emotions, particularly, anger and sadness.

Behavior patterns

Many who self-harm use multiple methods. Cutting arms or legs is the most common practice. Self-injurers may attempt to conceal the resultant scarring with clothing; and if discovered, often make excuses as to how an injury happened. A significant number are also struggling with eating disorders and alcohol or substance abuse problems. An estimated one-half to two-thirds of self-injurers have an eating disorder.

Reasons for the behavior

Self-injurers commonly report they feel empty inside, over or under stimulated, unable to express their feelings, lonely, not understood by others and fearful of intimate relationships and adult responsibilities. Self-injury is their way to cope with or relieve painful or hard-to-express feelings and is generally not a suicide attempt. But relief is temporary, and a self-destructive cycle often develops without proper treatment.

Evaluation

If someone displays the signs and symptoms of self-injury, a mental health professional with self-injury expertise should be consulted. An evaluation or assessment is the first step, followed by a recommended course of treatment to prevent the self-destructive cycle from continuing.

Diagnoses

The diagnosis for someone who self-injures can only be determined by a licensed psychiatric professional. Self-harm behavior can be a symptom of several psychiatric illnesses: Personality Disorders (esp. Borderline Personality Disorder); Bipolar Disorder (Manic-Depression); Major Depression; Anxiety Disorders (esp. Obsessive-Compulsive Disorder); as well as psychoses such as Schizophrenia.

WARNING SIGNS

- Unexplained frequent injuries, including cuts and burns
- Low self-esteem
- Wearing long pants and sleeves in warm weather
- Overwhelmed by feelings
- Inability to function at home, school or work
- Inability to maintain stable relationships

Dangers

Self-injurers often become desperate about their lack of self-control and the addictive-like nature of their acts, which may lead them to true suicide attempts. The self-injury behaviors may also cause more harm than intended, which could result in medical complications or death. Eating disorders and alcohol or substance abuse intensify the threats to the individual's overall health and quality of life.

Treatment and referral

If the initial evaluation determines that psychological intervention is warranted, the next step is to determine the level of care most appropriate for that particular student. Some schools have mental health professionals (e.g., school psychologists, social workers, counselors) available to conduct individual and/or group therapy for a prescribed amount of time. Most schools, however, do not have these resources available to them. In that case, a referral to professionals outside the school would need to be made.

Treatment options can include:

1. Outpatient individual therapy

2. Outpatient group therapy

3. Intensive outpatient (IOP) 2-3 hours a day for 2-5 days a week

4. Partial hospitalization (PHP) 6 hours a day

5. Inpatient or residential hospitalization. When the behaviors interfere with daily living, such as school and relationships, and are health or life-threatening, a specialized self-injury hospital program with an experienced staff is recommended.

The effective treatment of self-injury is most often a combination of medication, cognitive/behavioral therapy, and interpersonal therapy, supplemented by other treatment services as needed. Medication is often useful in the management of depression, anxiety, obsessive-compulsive behaviors, and the racing thoughts that may accompany self-injury. Cognitive-behavioral therapy helps individuals understand and manage their destructive thoughts and behaviors. Contracts, journals and behavior logs are useful tools for regaining self-control. Interpersonal therapy assists individuals in gaining insight and skills for the development and maintenance of relationships. Services for eating disorders, alcohol/substance abuse, trauma/abuse, and family therapy should be readily available and integrated into treatment, depending on individual needs.

In addition to the above, successful courses of treatment are marked by:

1) Clients who are actively involved in and committed to their treatment

2) Aftercare plans with support for the client's new self-management skills and behaviors

3) Collaboration with referring and other involved professionals

Section III

INTERVENTIONS

TEACHER PROTOCOL

What to Do When You Suspect That a Student is Injuring

Teachers are frequently the first adults to know of a student's self-injurious behavior. They may notice wounds, or may be notified by another student. On occasion, a student will decide to disclose to a teacher whom they trust. When a staff member notices that a student has wounds, suspects that a student is injuring or has the behavior brought to their attention by another student, the situation must be addressed and not ignored. One of the most important things to remember is that the tone of your response can be equally or even more important than your actual words. The goal is to respond in a calm, non-judgmental fashion.

Teachers often believe that self-injury is out of their area of expertise and are hesitant to become involved.

- **Myths:** **"If I ignore the behavior, it will go away."**
  "If I attend to the behavior, it will only encourage them to do it more."

  Many people, including teachers believe that self-injury is designed as an attention seeking behavior and therefore choosing to attend will only reinforce the behavior.

- **Reality: In general, it is *always* better to attend to the behavior rather than to ignore it.**

  Self-injury is an attempt to cope with a problem and not the problem itself. It is often a cry for help (either conscious or unconscious). Most self-injurers experience themselves as being invisible. Ignoring the behavior only validates this belief, possibly causing them to become even more dangerous to themselves. The key is to focus on the underlying feelings and issues rather than focusing on the behavior itself.

Don't be afraid to state, I've noticed cuts that appear to be self-inflicted, I care about why you might be doing that or, It appears you have hurt yourself, do you want to talk about it?". Even if the student denies that the wounds are self-inflicted, the fact that the behavior was attended to and addressed directly is the first step towards healing. You have made it clear that they are not invisible and that you are available when the student is ready to seek help.

If you believe that a student is self-injuring, let them know that you want to aid them in getting the help they need. It is most important to be empathic with the student. Remember, the self abuser may be feeling shame and you do not want to further this shame. Please DO NOT reprimand or send the student to the principal as a behavioral problem. Instead, your concerns should be brought to the attention of the school counselor if one is available to you. If your school does not have access to a counselor, you and/or the school nurse (depending on your school's protocol) will need to assess the student for safety (see page 36), especially if suicidal thoughts accompany the self injurious behavior. Explore other choices the student could have made, including the use of the Impulse Control Log© and alternatives (See pages 86 87)

If the student has fresh wounds, they will need to be assessed by the school nurse and/or emergency room to determine severity and to make sure that the wound is properly treated Our practice is to not focus on the injury, but rather on the events, feelings and thoughts preceding and following injuring.

What to Do When a Student has Recently Injured

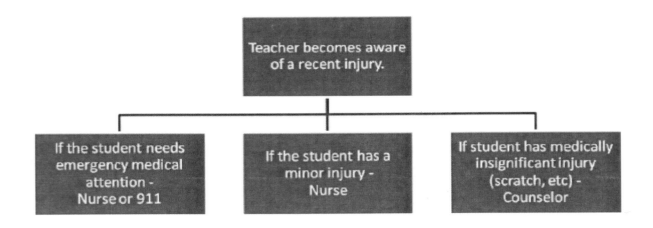

Figure 1

Serious, life threatening injury

If the student has hurt themselves seriously (e.g., cut an artery), notify the school nurse and call 911 immediately for an ambulance. The nurse will then notify the parents. Initial evaluation will take place in the emergency room

Minor injury

Unless the injury is very minor (e.g., skin scratch, eraser burn, etc.) the student should be sent to the school nurse for medical evaluation and wound care. The nurse will then complete a medical evaluation and treat the wound if necessary, and then accompany the student to the school counselor if available.

Minor injury or no fresh injury: no medical assessment necessary

If the student admits to the behavior, you can arrange to have them meet with the school counselor if one is available. Sometimes a counselor is not immediately available or the student just starts giving you information because they have a trusting relationship with you. In that case, you should understand and consider the following things when speaking with a student who is confiding in you about their self-injurious behavior.

· **Is this a one-time incident or have they injured before?**

It is important to ask if they have injured before, even if they don't tell you the truth. If they have injured previously, it is important to find out how frequently, all forms of injury and when they injured for the first time. It can also be informative to know if they can identify the precipitant to their first injury.

· **Does anyone know that they injure? Who?**

It may be that they have tried to tell someone (e.g., a pastor, friend, relative), but nothing happened. If they have told friends at the same school, those friends might benefit from counseling as this information can present a substantial emotional burden.

· **Did they self-injure because a friend injures?**

You can ask if they remember the first time they injured. Had they ever known anyone who injured prior to engaging in the behavior themselves? If they injured because a friend did it, why did they choose to do it too? (e.g., friend told them it worked...then ask the student " How did you hope it would work for you?" or " What were you hoping to achieve by injuring?")

- **Does their story sound reasonable as to how they got cuts, scratches or burns?**

  For instance, if they say the cat scratched them, but all the scratches are evenly spaced and the same length on the inside of the arm, it would be unlikely to have been created by a cat.

- **If they seemed unconcerned:**

  Inquire as to whether their friends or anyone else in their life have expressed concern. If they say yes, ask why they think their friends are concerned.

Some schools unfortunately do not have a school counselor available. The teacher or school nurse (depending on your school's protocol) will then have a major role in getting help for the student (See figure 2). In that case, the teacher/nurse should read the section designed for counselors as it gives direction for assessment, intervention, and notification of parents.

TEACHER DOs and DON'Ts

Response to self-injury

S.A.F.E. ALTERNATIVES®
Self Abuse Finally Ends

Don't
Ignore the behavior or unexplained injuries.
Do not address the issue in front of other students.

Do
Let the student know that you have noticed cuts that seem self-inflicted and that you are concerned and available to assist them in getting help. Make sure that you have this conversation in a private, confidential setting.

Don't
Threaten or punish the student. Don't send them to the principal or embarrass them in front of their peers.

Do
Let the student know that you are concerned about them and want to get them the help that they need. Facilitate a meeting with the school counselor if one is available.

Fresh wounds

Don't
Take care of the wounds yourself. Any wounds need to be cleaned and dressed and medically assessed by the nurse.

Do
Make sure the student is seen immediately by the school nurse.
Follow school protocol for cleaning up any blood in the classroom, bathroom, hallway, etc.
Make sure that other students are protected from coming into contact with open wounds or blood.

Boundaries

Don't
Cross boundaries by making promises you can't/shouldn't keep. For example, don't tell students that you will keep their injuries confidential from everyone (including school nurse, principal, parents, etc.).
Don't promise to be there 24/7, or give the impression that you are the only one who can help them.
Don't tell them all about your own emotional problems (e.g., addictions, depression, etc.).

Do
Maintain personal boundaries. Focus on the student's issues, not your own.
Accept your limitations and get the teen help they need, including the school counselor or outside referrals if that is in your purview.

SCHOOLS WITHOUT A SCHOOL COUNSELOR

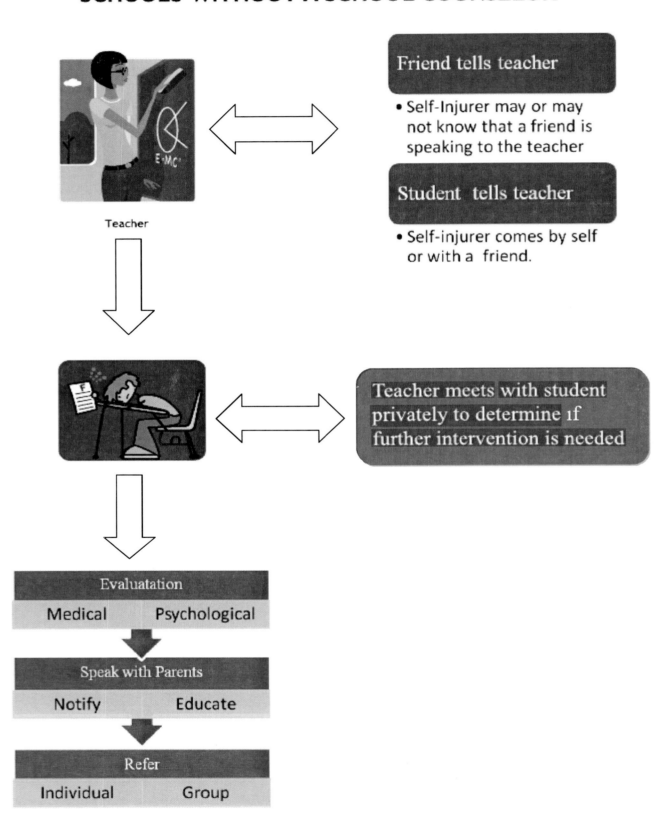

Teacher

Friend tells teacher

- Self-Injurer may or may not know that a friend is speaking to the teacher

Student tells teacher

- Self-injurer comes by self or with a friend.

Teacher meets with student privately to determine if further intervention is needed

Evaluatation

Medical   Psychological

Speak with Parents

Notify   Educate

Refer

Individual   Group

Figure 2

SCHOOL NURSE PROTOCOL
Emotional / medical response to injuries

S.A.F.E. ALTERNATIVES®
Self Abuse Finally Ends

Don't

Express strong emotional reactions to seeing a self-inflicted wound. Even though seasoned nurses have acknowledged such reactions, it is important to keep these feelings to oneself. Intense emotional reactions can also be exhibited through over determined responses such as excessive caretaking, anger or minimization.

Do

Listen calmly. Respond in a non-judgmental, non-blaming way. Take care of any wounds in a professional manner. Educate the student as to the dangers (i.e., infection, disease) of sharing or using otherwise unclean implements.

Questions about the incident

Don't

Ask questions in an accusatory fashion. Even simple questions can come across as judgments depending on tone and tenor. For example, don't ask, Why did you do that? Many teens will feel guilty enough about the behavior and will experience that type of question as a put down. In addition, they may have only a rudimentary idea, if that, as to why they engage in self-injurious behavior.

Do

Ask any questions in a caring and calm voice. They should be presented in such a way as to have the student think about the reasons for their behavior, rather than assume that they know the answer. (e.g., What is your understanding of self-injury? Do you have an idea of why you injured today?)

Alternatives

Don't

Teach replacement behaviors (e.g., snapping a rubber band on the wrist, squeezing an ice cube) that inflict pain in other ways.

Do

Teach ways to self soothe, (e.g., journaling, talking to a friend or school counselor) so they learn to tolerate painful feelings without resorting to injuring themselves.

Self-limitations

Don't

Make promises you can't keep. (e.g., to not tell anyone about the self-injury). You cannot rescue the student, nor should you try.

Do

Accept your own limitations. Follow up with referrals, and offers to go with the student to talk to the counselor, parents, etc., or to be there to listen.

PROVIDING A CARING ENVIRONMENT

Unstable, unpredictable or invalidating environments contribute to adolescent anxiety and frustration, which, in turn, can contribute to an increase in self-injurious impulses and injury. Therefore, stability and empathy are among the most important ingredients for success in working with self-injurers. Everyone in the system is responsible for providing a caring environment. Some descriptors of a caring environment are:

· Neutral: i.e., non-judgmental and non-punitive.

· Accepting: Staff can validate self-injurers' emotions. (A common theme among self-injurers is that their emotions were not validated during early family life).

· Amenable to staff contact. Since we want to encourage students to talk to staff about self-injurious impulses, staff can demonstrate openness to listening to them.

· Calm: Staff serves as models for emotional control, conflict-resolution and problem-solving skills.

· Dependable, structured and predictable (schedules, individual sessions, group time, consequences and/or expectations).

· Consistent and Neutral: Rules, rewards and consequences should be the same each day. Students should be apprised of any changes before they occur.

· Confidential and private: Staff refrains from discussing students when others are around and refrains from discussing sensitive issues with students (i.e., diagnosis, family conflict, etc.) in public (i.e., hallways, classroom).

· Safe: Staff members maintain appropriate boundaries and don't disclose personal information about their lives, etc. The information can become a burden to students. Instead, if they ask personal questions (e.g., whether you are married or have kids), ask why they asked that question. Why would it be important for you to know? You can also respond by asking What would it mean if I were married? or What would it mean to you if I were not married?

· Focused: Ask students to use the word self-injury versus cutting, burning, etc. Some people compete for the most dramatic type of self-injury. When everyone is a self-injurer, everyone is on the same level. Discouraging the display of scars or injuries helps to decrease contagion which is a major problem in schools. In addition, it keeps students focused on that which is truly important..... that is, the precipitant to the desire to injure, rather than the injury itself.

· Ask them to work on keeping themselves safe by completing and signing the form on page 63, Keeping Myself Safe.

SOME THINGS TO AVOID

- Don't give ultimatums (i.e., telling a student to not self-injure - or else!). Ultimatums rarely work and they threaten students' alliance with staff. Further, ultimatums result in the behavior going underground, serving to further alienate and shame the student, while also discouraging open and honest communication.

- Don't recommend substitute behaviors (i.e., snapping a rubber band attached to the wrist, submerging a limb in ice water or writing on the skin with markers). These strategies keep students focused on releasing tension through action and avoid reflecting on and managing underlying feelings. Some students also may use the substitute behavior to a degree that causes them harm.

- Avoid advocating the use of cathartic methods to express anger (i.e., punching a pillow). These behaviors focus the student on releasing tension through action and may distract the student from reflection. Self-injurers need to learn to calm themselves effectively. Students who self injure generally have difficulty self soothing. Cathartic methods escalate the anger rather than calming it.

- After the initial intervention, don't ask the student if they have injured unless the student needs medical attention for an injury. It is not advisable to conduct body checks, as this is infantilizing and represents a boundary violation. If however, there is reason to suspect a student has injured (e.g., fresh blood, etc.), it is reasonable for the nurse to evaluate the need for further care, prevent the transfer of blood to other students and notify the school counselor of ongoing self-injurious behavior.

SCHOOL COUNSELOR PROTOCOL

The school counselor can be one of the most important figures in the life of a student who self injurers. The way the counselor handles the first meeting, can often set the stage for that student's impression of the value of therapeutic intervention. The counselor has many jobs including assessment, education, intervention, referral, liaison and advocate.

A primary function, however, is to ensure the safety of the student. In order to accomplish that, the counselor needs to be able to assess and then determine and arrange appropriate intervention. Fostering an alliance with the student can help tremendously towards that end. However, as some teens view all adults as "clueless" authority figures who want to control or worse, take away a behavior that they may view as life saving, it is not always easy to accomplish. In our experience, if a student who self injures believes that you care about them (e.g., their thoughts and feelings) rather than just what they are doing (e.g., cutting, burning, etc.) you are much more likely to be successful in gaining their trust and obtaining more truthful responses.

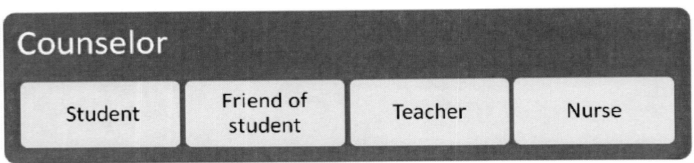

Figure 3

Assessing the Self Injurer for Suicidal Ideation

A student who self injures may come to a counselor's attention in a variety of ways (Fig.3) The student might approach the counselor directly, perhaps with the encouragement of a friend. The friend may come alone to tell the counselor about their concerns, with or without the self injurer's knowledge. A teacher may notice the signs of self injury and send a referral. The school nurse may be called in to check out or treat a wound and then bring the student for follow up counseling

Regardless of how a student arrives at your door, it is important to assess for imminent danger. A history of self-injury is a significant risk factor for suicide, so the behavior should be taken seriously each and every time it occurs. Therefore, even if a student has a history of non-suicidal self-injury, you should assess for imminent danger each time their self-injurious behavior comes to your attention.

Things to consider when assessing for level of danger:

1. **What does the student tell you about their intent?**

   Not all students will be honest, but it is important to ask what they were trying to accomplish with the behavior. Ask them directly if they intended to kill themselves. Even if they weren't attempting suicide, ask if they have ever had thoughts about suicide. If so, ask them if they have a plan about how they would kill themselves. If they answer yes, ask if they have the means to follow through. For example, if they state that they would shoot themselves, ask about access to a gun.

2. **Where on their body did they injure?**

   Are they injuring in lethal (e.g., wrists, femoral artery) or non-lethal areas (e.g., tops of arms, stomach, legs, etc.) of their bodies?

3. **How severe is the injury?**

   Even if the student did not intend to kill themselves, some injuries may cause permanent damage or even death.

4. **How do they injure?**

   In our experience, most people who attempt suicide use a method that is different, and usually more lethal, than their regular method of self-injury. So, for example, instead of cutting or burning, they may take pills.

You may use the following form to aid in your assessment.

Suicidal vs. Non-Suicidal Self-Injury Assessment

Name_____

Grade_____Date_____

S.A.F.E. ALTERNATIVES®
Self Abuse Finally Ends

Have you ever engaged in any of the following behaviors?

☐ Cut your skin with a knife or other sharp object?

☐ Burned yourself with a cigarette or other hot object?

☐ Pulled out your hair?

☐ Hit yourself with your hand or another object?

☐ Bitten yourself?

☐ Started a fight so you could get hurt?

☐ Engaged in an athletic sport in an effort to get hurt?

☐ Other_____

If you answered yes to any of the above, please state how often you engage in each behavior.

_____
_____
_____
_____

How old were you when you first self-injured? _____
How old are you now? _____

Have you told anyone that you injure   ☐ Yes   ☐ No

If yes, who have you told? Check all that apply:

☐ Mother   ☐ Father   ☐ Sister/Brother   ☐ Friend   ☐ Clergy

Have you ever been in therapy?   ☐ Yes   ☐ No

If yes, did/does your therapist know about the self-injury?
☐ Yes ☐ No

Have you ever thought about suicide? ☐ Yes ☐ No

If yes, have you ever told anyone about these thoughts?
☐ Yes ☐ No If yes, who did you tell? _____

If yes, have you ever considered how you would do it?
☐ Yes ☐ No

If yes, what was/is your plan? _____
_____
_____

Have you ever attempted suicide? ☐ Yes ☐ No

When?_ _____
_____
_____

Has anyone in your family ever attempted suicide?
☐ Yes ☐ No

If yes, who? _____

Have you experienced any recent stressor in your life (e.g., friends, family, school, sports, etc.) _____
_____
_____

Who is in your support system?
Family _____
Friends _____
Religious affiliation? _____ Is this important to you? _____

Determination:_____

Staff signature_____ Date _____

WHO SHOULD BE NOTIFIED?

Each school will have a different reporting structure Some schools have a counseling or social work department with several staff members and a department head. Other schools share a counselor with multiple other schools in their district. Thus, each school will need to determine their own protocol as to who needs to be notified when a student is identified as a self injurer. Figure 4 displays a sample reporting structure. Other potential persons to be notified will depend on the size of the school and the levels of administration. However, confidentiality is very important and should be breached on a need to know basis only.

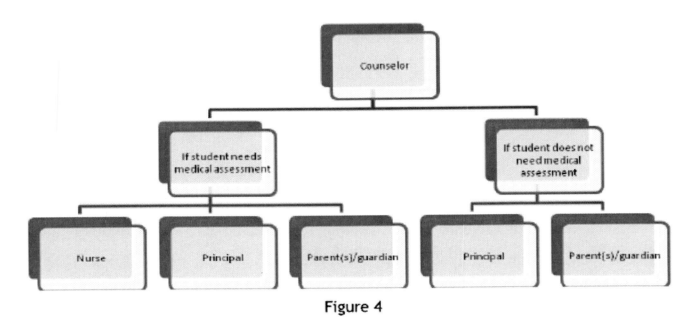

Figure 4

TALKING TO THE STUDENT ABOUT SELF INJURY

Students come to counselors in all stages of denial and/or readiness for help. Some are coerced by friends, teachers or another staff member, while others come on their own hoping for help. The counselor's approach may be influenced by this stage of readiness.

Students who come willingly to disclose their injurious behavior

1 It is important to tell the student that you are glad that they are aware of the problem and are seeking help because this is the first step towards recovery.
2 Assess for current suicidal thoughts and intent, as well as a history of suicide attempts, thoughts, intent Inquire about their family history of suicide, depression, substance abuse.

3. Ask the student about their understanding of self-injury. Students will display a wide range of understanding about why they injure. Some students won't have any idea why they injure. Others might have an understanding of the current precipitant (e.g., my boyfriend broke up with me), but little understanding of the larger picture (e.g., why they choose to injure under stress while others with the same stress don't injure).

  · Do they remember the first time they injured?

  · Do they recall why they started injuring?

  · Did they know anyone who injured before they did?

  · Did they think about injuring before they actually did so?

  · Have they told anyone else about their self-injurious behavior
    (e.g., parents, friends, clergy, online chat rooms, etc.)?

4. Explore counseling resources available to the student. Counselors generally have a referral list. However, it is important to find out which counselors on your list have experience/training in working with self-injury and have a desire to work with this population. A list of therapists from many areas of the country can be found at www.selfinjury.com. If there is an appropriate support group in school or the community, the student and parents may be informed of this and urge the student to attend. Your role of meeting with the student and parents will, of course, change if there is a school counselor employed by the school.

5. Ask them if they think they are able to keep themselves safe. If they say yes, have them complete and sign the form, Keeping Myself Safe on page 63. This form will help them to make plans for their own safety. While signing a piece of paper in no way ensures safety, it does help students to think about what they can do in the event of impulses, increasing the likeliness that they will maintain safety. If they are unable to sign this contract, they may need a higher level of care, up to and including hospitalization.

6. Assist in developing a safety plan. The student can be given tools as to what they can do when an impulse to injure presents itself, e.g., utilizing their alternatives (page 84) and the Impulse Control Log® (page 86).

Students who are reported by friends or referred by a teacher but deny the fact that they injure:

1. Ask the student why they think their teacher or friend referred them to the counseling department.

2. Ask them if they engage in any behavior that others would consider self-injurious, even if they don't.

3. If they answer yes to the above question, ask if they would be concerned if their younger sibling (or friend, younger cousin, etc.) engaged in similar behavior.

4. Ask them if they can make a promise to keep themselves safe. If so, have them sign the Keeping Myself Safe form on page 63.

Students who are caught in the act and brought in by a nurse or a teacher:

1. Inquire about the precipitating event. Why now, what thoughts were they having just prior to the injurious act

2. How are they feeling now?

3. How often do they injure?

4. Have they ever told anyone that they injure?

5. Have they ever been (or are they currently) in therapy for this or any other concerns? If they are in therapy you should consider obtaining a release of information so that you can let the therapist know how the student is doing in school, and hopefully collaborate on a treatment plan.

Use the Process Questions (page 49) to help them understand what happened. Ask them if they think they are able to keep themselves safe. If they say yes, ask them to complete and sign the form, Keeping Myself Safe (page 63). If they say no, assess for level of danger (page 36) and make an appropriate referral.

S.A.F.E. ALTERNATIVES®
Self Abuse Finally Ends

STRATEGIES FOR HELPING SELF-INJURERS

Do	Don't
Help to see the consequences of his/her behavior/choices	Engage in power struggles
Model the ability to handle stress	Collude with helplessness by panicking with the self-injurer
Help to tolerate/accept uncomfortable feelings	Make promises you can't keep (e.g., you will keep them safe)
Try to understand and validate the meaning behind the behavior and help the student to communicate needs more directly	Belittle the struggle (it's only for attention)
Help students express anger non-violently	Use cathartic methods such as punching bags, hitting pillows, etc.
Focus on issues that precipitate an impulse to injure	Use substitute behaviors (snapping rubber bands, ice water, etc.)

HELPING STUDENTS DISCLOSE TO PARENT(S)

It is our opinion, if the student is under the age of 18, the parent(s) should be contacted. Frequently, a child who self-injures states that they do not want their parents to know that they are injuring. It is very important to get a better understanding of why the child does not want their parent(s) to be contacted. In some instances, the self injury may be a reflection of the stress or abuse experienced at home. Parents can be a critical part of the recovery process, but only if they are well-informed and supportive.

Teens almost always fear that their parents will be disappointed, angered or perhaps overwhelmed by the news of their child's self-injurious behavior. Some parents do, in fact, react inappropriately, such as responding with anger, threatening to ground their children or take away prized possessions such as phone, TV or music; while others minimize the problem believing that it is a fad. Others become overwhelmed and hysterical, wanting to admit their child to a hospital. Most often, these types of reactions stem from fear or ignorance. In some cases, however, the student may fear retribution from an abusive parent.

1. **Explore student's fears of disclosing the self-injury to their parents and help them to not take responsibility for their parent's response.**

    Ask clarifying questions such as:

    How do you think your parent(s) will react when they find out that you are injuring?
    What is your worst fear about them knowing?

    What will it mean to you if your parent(s) is _____ (e.g., angry, scared, disappointed, hurt, etc?)?

IMPORTANT

Using the above questions, determine whether the student is in fear of a physical (abusive) response. If the student discloses past parental abuse, then Child Protective Services (CPS or comparable agency in your area) will need to be notified. While not all parents of self-injurers are abusive, it is more common in this population than in the general student body, so professionals need to be extremely sensitive and educated about domestic violence, including sexual abuse.

2. **Help them understand their own feelings about their behavior which may interfere with telling their parents (e.g., shame, normalization).**

   The first step towards health is to disclose their secret and to identify their feelings.

3. **Help them to work through their fears (e.g., that people will think they are crazy).**

4. **Encourage the student to tell their parents themselves.**

   The best scenario is for the child to make the phone call with you. Let them know that you will be there as their advocate and will help to educate the family on self harm and refer them to appropriate treatment. If the student refuses to tell, you can have her/him wait somewhere else while you speak with her/his parents. This is also an opportunity to check on problems at home.

GOALS FOR PARENT MEETING

To schedule a meeting with parents

While the first contact will likely be by phone, it may be important to meet with the parents in person. How available vs. resistant the parents are to meeting with you will give you a better idea of what the student may encounter at home. Many parents may think that self-injury is a reflection on their failings as a parent and become defensive. How you deal with the parent(s) will serve as a role model for the student. It is important to not be intimidated by angry parents and not respond with aggression or hopelessness to parents who display a lack of understanding or worse, indifference. Instead, remain professional and consistent.

To educate parents about health and psychological risks associated with self-injury

Parents need to understand the potential risks of infection and permanent scars, but more importantly to understand that injuring is a coping strategy and not the problem itself. Instead of focusing on the behavior, they need to understand that their child needs help to identify and express their emotional discomforts verbally, rather than expressing them through behaviors. You may want to show them a video such as Can You See my Pain or CUT and recommend that they read the book *Bodily Harm* (Conterio & Lader). All are available in the store at selfinjury.com.

To help parents deal with their own emotional response

Parents may respond with anger or they may minimize the problem, stating that their child is just doing it for attention. Let them know that self-injury is never a healthy coping strategy and that it is an indication that their child is having trouble coping with stressful issues and emotions.

If the parents hesitate to take the problem seriously, recommend that they get a professional assessment to make the determination. Let them know that adolescents often do not confide in their parents and might be more open with a professional counselor. Caution them about overreacting which can result in the child hiding their behavior.

To help them accept their own reactions

Fear, anger and guilt are all normal reactions and should be accepted as such. Parents can process them and find a way to remain understanding toward their adolescent. Help them to understand that their child is likely in a great deal of emotional pain that he/she has not been able to express directly.

To provide reassurance

As a family, they most likely have overcome many things and they can overcome this issue as well. Stress the fact that their adolescent has the resilience needed to help him/her through this challenging period.

To encourage parents to have appropriate expectations

Parents may be eager to talk to their son/daughter about self-injury, but their teen may be reticent. Adolescents generally find it very difficult to identify, much less discuss, feelings and issues that underlie self-injury. It will take time and work before they can identify and communicate their feelings.

To tell them not to expect to fix the problem

Their adolescent is in need of a professional assessment and possibly treatment. Parents can be available to listen and empathize.

To encourage parents not to threaten or overprotect their teen in an attempt to stop the behavior

Entering into a power struggle in an effort to control a youth's behavior rarely works and often results in an exacerbation rather than a reduction in the intensity and/or frequency of the behavior. Parents can, however, make their self-injuring teen become more aware of the possible consequences of the behavior (e.g., loss of friendships, permanent scars). If parents suspect self-injury, they should openly express their concern for their adolescent, indicate they want to help and encourage their teen to talk to them or another trusted adult (e.g., school counselor, religious leader, relative) who can then help them get professional help if warranted. If the parent observes an actual injury, the parent can, if necessary, transport them to the emergency room or doctor's office.

To instruct them not to hesitate to seek help, (e.g., therapy or hospitalization) for their child

Parents will not be betraying their child by seeking help. Instead, they will model a healthy parental attitude, demonstrating they can accept problems and deal with them constructively. It is important for them to know that adolescents often do not confide in their parents and might be more willing to be open with a professional counselor.

To encourage parents to find their own therapy and support system

Having a teen that self-injures affects the entire family. Therapy can help both parents and siblings deal with their own emotional reactions to the self-injurious behavior, as well as to the self-injurer her/himself. It is important for family members to be able to identify and express their own feelings in healthy ways, so they don't start walking on eggshells, or exploding as a result of keeping their own feelings bottled up. Parents can learn to monitor their own communication skills and thus model healthy styles of both affect tolerance and communication. Family therapy can be especially productive to this end, as it will focus on evaluation and improvement of communication within the family.

To help them understand not to expect a quick cure
It takes some time for the self-injurer's pattern to develop and it will likely take time to heal.

IF PARENTS BELIEVE THEIR CHILD IS SUICIDAL

Parents should immediately contact the adolescent's therapist if they have one, take their teen to the nearest emergency room or call 911. While most adolescents who self-injure are not trying to attempt suicide, self-injury is a strong risk factor for suicide. Therefore, if someone is making suicidal statements, they must be taken seriously.

WHEN THE SELF-INJURER REFUSES TREATMENT

Parents may have to deal with a reluctant teenager. If she/he denies the behavior is a problem, parents can tell the child that, if true, the belief will be confirmed by a consultation with a professional. It's important to provide choices of where to get help and ask the adolescent to select one. This way, the youth experiences some control and a power struggle is less likely to develop.

If the student is in denial of the severity of the problem, ask them to complete the Self-Injury Self Assessment form on page 57. Even if they are not willing to share the answers with you, they may gain a new perspective of their behavior.

REFERRALS

Counselors will need to make the determination as to when a student should be referred to outside therapy. As noted earlier in this text (page 21), the counselor will need to determine the level of care needed including whether to divest themselves of the care of the student entirely or to continue to provide partial treatment for the student. Much of that will depend on the options available to the student within the school (e.g., group therapy, availability of counselors, etc.) as well as the desires of the outside counselor. Students who injure may become attached quickly to a person who lends an empathic ear and has offered their assistance. It is therefore important, that should a referral be made, the student understands that this is done out of caring rather than anger, or frustration.

Counselors should know the therapists they refer to, understand their philosophy of treatment and expertise and training in working with those who self-injure. Visits to local partial hospital or inpatient programs are recommended so that you have a working knowledge of the intake procedure, as well as what the various facilities have to offer. It is also advantageous to know how the facility works with the school, and how the student's educational needs will be met while in one of their programs.

SCHOOL ACCOMMODATIONS & TRANSITIONS AFTER TREATMENT

If it becomes necessary for a student to attend an outside treatment program there will be in an indefinite absence from school. The school counselor will need to work closely with the treatment team to ensure continuity of care and education. The counselor may be asked to attend a team conference at the program. Be aware that parents may be reluctant to have you know too much about their child's emotional difficulties, diagnoses, medications, etc., as they fear issues of confidentiality and prejudice once the child returns to school. You may have to reassure the parents that having information about the child's psychological and medical needs will aid in the return to school and ensure that every one is on board with the agreed on treatment plan.

The School Transition Plan (page 59) is useful to help students identify their fears about returning to school or to class if the self-injury has been known at school. They can ask for what they want or need from school in the way of support. The treatment team will decide on the Individual Accommodations (page 61). The counselor or assigned staff will follow up with notes and recommendations (page 62).

Transitioning back to school after treatment or intervention is often an overwhelming experience for adolescents, especially if the core issues/triggers are in the school setting. The following is a list of accommodations staff can make to ease the student into the system:

- Set up a communication system for the classroom (verbal or nonverbal) where the student can indicate he or she is having a problem.

- Offer support from social workers or teachers (assigned times to talk, check ins throughout the day, etc. Consistency and stability are important, so the assigned person should be someone who will be available at the assigned times).

- Teach the student to use the Impulse Control Log®, which the student should have with her/him at all times. This helps the student identify the feeling she/he may be experiencing and manage any impulses to self-injure.

- Encourage the student to use healthy ALTERNATIVES for coping with uncomfortable feelings rather than acting on them (i.e., using the Impulse Control Log®, journaling, etc.).

- Refer to treatment recommendations for information on interventions, medications, diagnoses and outpatient therapist and/or psychiatrist.

- Allow time for the student to work through any issues or conflicts in order to get back on track for school.

ADVOCACY and EDUCATION:

Advocacy and education are important roles for the school's mental health professionals. Helping teachers, nurses and administrators better understand the meanings of this behavior can help combat some of the myths that remain rampant about self-injurers (e.g., they just want attention, it's not a big deal, the behavior's not dangerous, everyone grows out of it.. it's just a fad, they're crazy or suicidal, etc.). Once staff is informed, they are more likely to acknowledge, identify and direct students to the counseling center for help. We recommend that in-services be provided to all school staff.

Education of the student body is also important. Our fact sheet can be distributed to students and parents alike. Friends of self-injurers often need support as well. They need to come to terms with their own limitations, learn to set limits without guilt and learn how to refer their self-injuring friends to the school counseling office.

S.A.F.E. ALTERNATIVES*
Self Abuse Finally Ends

Process Questions

Self-injury is an impulsive act. Answering these questions will give you an opportunity to think about the incident and the response you chose to make.

Self injury is a way of displacing feelings from the head to the body. You may have trouble identifying feelings. A feeling list is provided to help you identify what you are feeling. Feelings are valuable clues to what needs to be looked at, worked through and resolved. The ability to sit with feelings and not be overwhelmed is a strong sign of recovery.

To help understand what happened or has been happening, please answer the following questions:

What did you...

Think? _____

_____

_____

_____

_____

_____

Feel?_____

_____

_____

_____

_____

_____

Believe? _____

_____

_____

_____

_____

_____

Want? _____

_____

_____

_____

_____

_____

Need? _____

_____

_____

_____

_____

_____

Choose? _____

_____

_____

_____

_____

_____

Until you are able to manage your impulses, it is very important to have support from people you trust. Please look at the Keeping Myself Safe form on page 49 in the *Student Workbook*, fill it out and sign it in the presence of someone you trust.

S.A.F.E. ALTERNATIVES® Impulse Control Log® – Side 1

ACTING OUT/SELF INJURY THOUGHTS: (e.g., cutting, running away)	TIME AND DATE: (e.g., 9:00 P.M. 2/15/0?)	LOCATION: (e.g., bedroom)	SITUATION: (e.g., I was by myself, thinking about getting better.)	FEELING: (e.g., scared)	WHAT WOULD BE THE RESULT OF SELF-INJURY? (e.g., more scars loss of trust of family /friends)

S.A.F.E. ALTERNATIVES® Impulse Control Log® – Side 2

WHAT WOULD I BE TRYING TO COMMUNICATE WITH MY SELF-INJURY? (e.g., I'm scared and I need attention.)	ACTION TAKEN: How were thoughts/feelings communicated or coped with? (e.g., I used my five alternatives and confronted my distorted thoughts.)	OUTCOME: (e.g., I noticed a decrease in my desire to act out.)

S.A.F.E. ALTERNATIVES®
Self Abuse Finally Ends

Confrontation Log®
(See Workbook page 16, Manual page 70)

Learning to Confront Effectively

What is a confrontation? A confrontation is the act of stating one's opinion in order to bring about change, or the act of challenging one's own negative thinking.

> Example 1: *Telling another person that you experienced their behavior or comment as destructive/abusive.*

> Example 2: *Challenge means to call into question as to why you think you are "bad", "stupid", "need to be punished", etc...*

Who are you confronting and why? _____

_____

How do you plan to confront this person(s) and when? _____

_____

What do you hope to accomplish by confronting this person(s)?_____

_____

_____

Outcome of confrontation _____

_____

What did you learn about yourself from this confrontation?_____

_____

Negative thoughts about yourself _____

_____

What questions or challenges did you ask of yourself?_____

_____

What did you learn about yourself from this challenge? _____

_____

_____

S.A.F.E. ALTERNATIVES®
Self Abuse Finally Ends

Dilemma Log®
(See Workbook page 17, Manual page 70)

What is a dilemma? A dilemma is an undesirable or unpleasant conflict.

> Example: *A friend just told you something that could cause harm and asked you to not tell anyone.*

Write down your dilemma.

_____
_____
_____

Write down your thoughts regarding your dilemma _____
_____

How are you dealing with your dilemma? _____
_____
_____
_____

Have you shared your dilemma with anyone? Yes___ No___

    If yes, with whom? _____
    If no, why not? _____

Have you decided on an outcome scenario for your dilemma? Yes___ No___
    If yes, is this outcome realistic? Yes___ No___
Do you find yourself ruminating over this outcome? Yes___ No___ NA___

Outcome:
What steps will you take when a dilemma arises? _____
_____

What have you learned about how you deal with dilemmas? _____
_____
_____

S.A.F.E. ALTERNATIVES®
Self Abuse Finally Ends

Productive Risk Taking Log®

(See Workbook page 18, Manual page 71)

Productive risk taking is acting on or verbally communicating a need or a concern which is out of one's comfort zone.

Example: *Setting a limit, or saying "no" to a friend.*

Describe the risk. _____

_____

_____

Write your fear(s) about this risk: _____

_____

_____

How do you plan to take this risk and when? _____

_____

_____

What do you hope to accomplish by taking this risk? _____

_____

OUTCOME:

Describe how the risk turned out. _____

_____

_____

_____

Describe how the risk turned out:_____

What did you learn about yourself by taking this risk?_____

_____

_____

_____

S.A.F.E. ALTERNATIVES®
Self Abuse Finally Ends

Negative Thinking Log®

(See Workbook page 19, Manual page 71)

Challenging negative thinking means to call into question one's own beliefs or thoughts.

Example:

Question/Statement: *Why do I think of myself as "bad"? Or "I am stupid" or "I need to be punished", etc...*

Belief: *I think I am bad because I caused my parents to divorce.*

Challenge: *Maybe my parents just could not get along, and their divorce had nothing to do with me.*

Question/Statement: _____

Belief: _____

Challenge: _____

Question/Statement: _____

Belief: _____

Challenge: _____

Question/Statement: _____

Belief: _____

Challenge: _____

Question/Statement: _____

Belief: _____

Challenge: _____

SELF-INJURY
SELF ASSESSMENT*

S.A.F.E. ALTERNATIVES*
Self Abuse Finally Ends

1. I was often told as a child that I had to be strong.	True_____	False_____
2. I do not remember much affection being displayed in my family.	True_____	False_____
3. Anger was the feeling most often displayed in my family.	True_____	False_____
4. I rarely felt I could express my feelings to my family.	True_____	False_____
5. As a child I remember my mother and/or father as overly intrusive.	True_____	False_____
6. As a child I remember being sexually abused.	True_____	False_____
7. As a child I remember being physically abused.	True_____	False_____
8. As a child I remember being emotionally abuse.	True_____	False_____
9. As a child my mother and/or father was emotionally absent.	True_____	False_____
10. I remember times when I was punished for strong feelings.	True_____	False_____
11. When I was upset or frightened, I was ignored.	True_____	False_____
12. I grew up in a very religious household.	True_____	False_____
13. I had a parent who was unable to raise me due to a physical illness or trauma.	True_____	False_____
14. I grew up with a lot of double messages.	True_____	False_____
15. I often think of myself as a —bad‖ person.	True_____	False_____
16. I often believe that I'm at fault for everything that goes wrong.	True_____	False_____
17. I often think that everyone would be happier if I were dead.	True_____	False_____
18. I hate change.	True_____	False_____
19. I seem to have an all-or-nothing attitude,	True_____	False_____
20. I usually can't find words that explain how I feel.	True_____	False_____
21. I am a perfectionist.	True_____	False_____
22. I think I am a burden to others.	True_____	False_____
23. I do not want to die; I just want to stop my emotional pain.	True_____	False_____
24. My friends and family have become concerned about my body piercing.	True_____	False_____
25. I have decided to continue piercing despite the fact that one or more significant others have told me that they are repulsed by it.	True_____	False_____
26. I become anxious when anyone tries to stop me or prevent me from getting a new piercing.	True_____	False_____
27. I have problems with drugs or alcohol.	True_____	False_____
28. I have sometimes neglected to seek medical attention for an illness or injury when part of me knows that I should have.	True_____	False_____
29 I have an eating disorder, or have had one sometime in the past.	True_____	False_____
30. I have – or have had- a tendency to be promiscuous.	True_____	False_____
31. I have overdosed on drugs.	True_____	False_____
32. I often obsess about self-injury.	True_____	False_____
33. I sometimes can't explain where my injuries come from.	True_____	False_____
34. I get anxious when my wounds start to heal.	True_____	False_____
35. I often believe that if I don't self-injure, I'll go —crazy.‖	True_____	False_____
36. No one can hurt me more than I can hurt myself.	True_____	False_____
37. I can't imagine life without self-injury.	True_____	False_____
38. If I stop self-injuring, my parents win.	True_____	False_____
39. I often self-injure as a way to punish myself.	True_____	False_____

40. Self-injury is my best friend.   True_____ False_____

41. I consider my tendency to self-harm an addiction.   True_____ False_____

42. Many times I harm myself more out of habit than for any specific
reason.   True_____ False_____

43. I have self-injured: Only once__ 2-5 times__ 6-10 times__11-20 times__ 21-50 times__
More than 50 times__

44. When did you last harm yourself? Within the past 6 weeks__ Past six months__ Past year__
More than one year ago__?

Questions 1-14

The more questions you answered "true", the more likely it is that your early experiences were similar to those described by self-injurers.

Questions 15-23

The more questions you answered "true" in this section, the more your view of yourself matches the views commonly expressed by self-injurers.

Questions 24-31

If you answered "true" to any of these questions, it may signal that you have a serious problem with self-injury.

Questions 32-44

We suggest that anyone who answered "true" to any of these questions might benefit from consultation with a professional who understands self-injury. You may use the questionnaire as a tool for discussion during the consultation.

If you would like to make an appointment for a phone screening (it will take approximately 1 hour), please contact us at:

800-DONTCUT (800-366-8288)

E-mail: info@selfinjury.com

Note: This assessment may be copied.

***This assessment is based on our clinical experience and not research.
It is meant to be used as a tool for self evaluation and not intended to diagnose.**

S.A.F.E. ALTERNATIVES®
Self Abuse Finally Ends

School Transition Plan

Name: _____

School and Grade: _____

Date: _____

As you prepare to return to the classroom, it is important that you have the support, guidance and resources to make the transition as smooth as possible. This form can help you prepare for your return to class. Remember, sometimes a return to class may be welcome, but it can also be overwhelming.

1. How can your social worker or guidance counselor support you when you return to class?

_____
_____
_____
_____
_____
_____
_____
_____
_____

2. How can your teachers support you when you return to class?

_____
_____
_____
_____
_____
_____
_____
_____

3. What are some of your social and emotional needs that should be addressed before returning to class?

_____
_____
_____
_____
_____
_____
_____

4. What ALTERNATIVES do you plan to use when having impulses to injure in class?

_____
_____
_____
_____
_____
_____
_____

5. Who are your support people to use at school?

_____
_____
_____
_____
_____
_____

6. What are some other changes that you would like to see happen at school?

_____
_____
_____
_____
_____
_____

7. What are your overall feelings about returning to class?

_____
_____
_____
_____
_____
_____

S.A.F.E. ALTERNATIVES®
Self Abuse Finally Ends

Individual Accommodations

Name: _____

School and Grade_____

Date_____Age_____

After completing a School Transition Plan, this student has requested the following accommodations to ease his or her transition back to school or classroom:

1.

2.

3.

4.

5.

SCHOOL NOTES and RECOMMENDATIONS

S.A.F.E. ALTERNATIVES®
Self Abuse Finally Ends

Name: _____

School and Grade_____

Date_____ Age_____

Severity of the problem: No problem_____ Mild_____ Moderate_____ Severe_____

Meeting with the student: Date_____Assessment outcome_____

_____

_____

Call to parents or guardian to set up appointment? _____ Date_____

Appointment Date_____

Recommendations

Type of treatment believed appropriate? _____

_____

_____

_____

Group Support? _____

Referred to? _____ Date: _____

_____

_____

Release of information for referral signed by parent(s) or guardian if student is under age 18? _____

NOTES: _____

_____

_____

_____

_____

_____

Staff Signature_____Date_____

Keeping Myself Safe

A promise to be discussed and signed
in front of someone you trust

S.A.F.E. ALTERNATIVES*
Self Abuse Finally Ends

Here are five things I can do if I have impulses to hurt
myself:

1._____

2._____

3._____

4._____

5._____

Here are three people I can call for support if I have impulses to hurt myself:

1._____

2._____

3._____

Instead of hurting myself, I can nurture myself by:

1._____

2._____

3_____

Your safety is our main concern. We want to be certain you are feeling safe. If you have thoughts of hurting yourself or someone else, please:

1) Call the hotline at 800-273-TALK
2) Call 911
3) Go to your nearest emergency room.

I understand that I need to contact 911 or go to the nearest emergency room if I want to hurt myself or someone else.

Signed_____**Date**_____

Witness_____ **Date**_____

Notes

"I count him braver who overcomes his desires than him who overcomes his enemies; for the hardest victory is victory over self." - **Aristotle**

Section IV

INSTRUCTIONS FOR USING THE STUDENT WORKBOOK

Student Workbook Contents

This section of the manual is designed to be used by professionals who work directly with children and adolescents who self-injure; it is coordinated with the Student Workbook. The purpose of the Student Workbook is to find a comfortable way for you to establish a relationship with students and ultimately, to help them identify the feelings and issues underlying their self-injury and to teach them new coping skills.

This workbook can be used as an individual intervention (e.g., given to a student to complete on their own and then review with a staff member) or as a format for a more in-depth individual session with a counselor or in small group settings. The exercises can be used randomly or in order. It is possible to pick and choose the parts of exercises that are relevant at a given time. We offer more than enough options so that you will be able to choose the best fit for you.

If there are several students engaging in self-injury, it can be beneficial to meet with them as a group. In group they can work on communication skills while reflecting on their own issues and those of their peers. The group must be a safe place for growth and change, as well as an arena for students to practice a new set of behaviors. Therefore, it is important to allow no comparison of injuries or graphic language about injuring. (Students may use the term self-injure but would not be allowed to describe specifics of the incident when talking with their peers.) Focus on the feelings before, during and after the act, rather than the act itself. If you decide to use the Student Workbook in a group setting, there are helpful guidelines on pages 109-112 in this Manual and pages 45-48 in the Workbook.

There are a variety of ways to help adolescents verbalize feelings in a non-threatening way. Writing assignments are meant to help organize thoughts on issues that often underlie self-injury. They also aid in developing self-awareness and identifying feelings that surround the issues. Students often state that writing makes things "more real". Art and music are other pathways to underlying feelings.

Using the exercises in the workbook will enable the staff to:

·   Validate that students are doing the best they can to survive, while at the same time, helping them to learn healthier and more productive ways of doing so.

·   Act as appropriate role models for social behaviors, being respectful of boundaries.

·   Develop a working relationship with students and families.

·   Learn how to assure student rights to privacy and confidentiality.

Student goals are to learn to:

- Accept responsibility for their choices, including self-injury.

- Address their defenses in an effort to identify and express their true feelings (core affect).

- Distinguish a thought, from a feeling, from an action.

- Tolerate uncomfortable feelings.

- Experience a feeling (e.g., anger) without an action (e.g., violence).

- Challenge irrational thoughts.

- Increase the window of opportunity between an impulse (thought) and an action (self-injury).

- Communicate thoughts and feelings to others in a verbal and appropriate manner.

- Face fears directly rather than medicating them through self-injury.

- Eliminate all self-injurious behaviors.

USING THE EXERCISES IN THE STUDENT WORKBOOK

Exercise 1: Process Questions and Alternatives
(See Workbook pages 7-10, Manual page 81)

Process Questions: Self-injury is an impulsive act. Answering the process questions gives a student the opportunity to think about the incident and the response they chose to make. This can be used for a current situation or one that has happened in the past; either is beneficial.

Feelings: Self-injury is a way of displacing feelings from the head to the body. Self-injurers usually cannot stand being alone with their feelings, and so they act out instead of looking at what is uncomfortable. They often cannot even identify what they are feeling and will say I feel like hurting myself or I feel like no one likes me!. Those are both thoughts, not feelings. A feeling list (page 83) is provided to help them identify what they are feeling. Feelings are valuable clues to what needs to be looked at, worked through and resolved. The ability to sit with feelings and not be overwhelmed is a strong sign of recovery.

Alternatives: These are temporary distractions to use when impulses are very strong and the student needs to get some emotional distance before she/he can process the impulse. Some therapists think that these alternatives can actually serve as a substitute for self-injury, *but they don't!* The only true solution is to face the underlying cause. Therefore, once a student uses these alternatives and gets some emotional distance, it is imperative that they complete one of the logs provided so as to better understand what precipitated the impulse and face that concern directly.

Students should choose alternatives that are possible while they are in school. For example, "cooking" would not work if they don't have access to ingredients or a stove. Examples of common alternatives would be: journaling, listening to music, doing an Impulse Control Log®, talking to a staff member or drawing, etc.

We give the space for 18 alternatives. At first they might only be able to come up with a few. We encourage them to start with at least five and add to the list as they discover other activities that they find enjoyable or soothing.

Exercise 2: Learning to use Logs
(See Workbook pages 11-20, Manual page 85)

It is recommended that one session be used to teach students to use the logs and another session focus on processing individual logs. Students will bring their Impulse Control Logs® and share difficult or challenging impulses. The focus is on their feelings and the alternative choices they made instead of injuring. Themes, patterns and triggers are discussed. The logs can all be introduced at once or you can let a student become comfortable with the Impulse Control Log® and then introduce the others. If used in a group setting, students may also present another S.A.F.E. log, if time allows. It is the responsibility of the staff member to monitor the group so that each member has time to share a log. The goal is that the writing will become a substitute for the behavior and, ultimately, the self-injurer will understand the connection between thoughts, feelings, and behaviors. Therefore, discourage them from doing the logs in their head.

Impulse Control Log® (Page 86): The Impulse Control Log® was designed to help think through impulses before choosing to act on them. It helps to focus on the reason *behind* the impulse to injure, rather than focusing on the impulse itself. The facilitator's job is to help recognize patterns to the impulses such as time of day, where the student was when they experienced the impulse, and precipitating event(s) (e.g., conflict with a parent or friend, nurse questioned the need for pain/anxiety meds, illness or death of a friend, etc.).

It is important to be specific on the log as global responses are not generally helpful. An example of a global entry would be *"My teacher made me very angry"* a better entry would be *"My teacher said that I talked too much and it made me mad"*. The goal is that the writing will become a substitute for the behavior and, ultimately, the self-injurer will understand the connection between thoughts, feelings, and behaviors. Therefore, discourage them from doing the logs in their head.

More Logs:
(See Workbook page 14, Manual page 88)

Once you have learned to use Impulse Control Logs® you might want to utilize one of the following more specific logs.

1. **Confrontation Log® (page 90)**

   This log helps one think through and manage confrontation. Confrontation is not pleasant for most of us; but for self-injurers, who often harbor tremendous fears of abandonment, confrontation can become particularly difficult. Since it is so difficult, people often respond in extremes: either avoiding confrontation all together; or confronting in a hostile, aggressive manner. The goal is to challenge irrational thoughts so that you are better able to assert needs in an appropriate manner.

2. **Dilemma Log® (page 91)**

   This log is designed to help think through dilemmas and challenge irrational/catastrophic thinking to come up with a healthy solution.

   Examples: *You are aware that a peer has self-injured. Do you tell, or do you keep the secret?*

You see another student cheating, do you tell?

Your best friend's boyfriend is cheating on her. Do you let her know?

This log helps the student to think through the consequences of each decision.

3. Productive Risk Taking Log® (page 92)

This log helps one plan an action or verbally communicate a need or concern that is out of one's comfort zone. People would rather tolerate their own misery than take a risk to change. Dwelling on a failed outcome often paralyzes people from taking a risk. This log helps one carefully plan strategies for moving on in his/her life.

· Preparing to take a risk is the first step.

> Example: *The risk may be to share something personal and painful. The fear is that your peers will think "badly" of you.*

· Next, ask the student how they want to proceed with the risk and when.

> Example: *I want to take this risk in group.*

· Identify what they hope to accomplish by taking this risk.

> Example: *That I may became closer to the group, that other peers will share similar experiences, and that regardless of the outcome I needed to share as a way to heal.*

· Record the outcome of the risk taken.

> Example: *They may say it was not as bad as they thought it would be, or that they were surprised at how others opened up because they opened up.*

· The last entry tells what they learned about themselves by taking this risk.

> Example: *They may learn that they do not have to be alone in their pain, that they have strengths, and most importantly, that they can expand their comfort zone with each risk.*

4. Negative Thinking Log® (page 93)

This log helps one organize how they think about themselves and challenge their belief system. Most people do not realize just how often negative thinking leads to self-injurious behavior. When asked to explore their thoughts, most self-injurers say they do not know how to think in ways that are not negative. This log guides one into thinking differently. Use these three steps when a negative thought arises.

- First, write down the negative <u>Question or Statement</u>

> Example: *"Why do I think of myself as "bad"?" or "I am stupid" or "I need to be punished" etc.?*

- Next, write down the <u>Belief.</u>

> Example: *"I think I"m "bad" because I caused my parents to divorce."*

- Lastly, <u>Challenge</u> these statements and beliefs.

> Example: *"Maybe my parents just could not get along, and their divorce had nothing to do with me."*

It will take time to become comfortable "logging" <u>and</u> it is worth the effort.

Exercise 3: How do I See Myself?
(See Workbook pages 21-22, Manual pages 94-95)

Goal: Identifying strengths and weaknesses

It is important for students to acknowledge both their positive and negative traits, and decide which ones enhance their ability to cope and which ones cause difficulties. By sharing this assignment with others, they can get feedback about whether their perceptions are accurate.

A List of MY Positive Qualities: A worksheet for students to list their strengths.

Exercise 4: Talking About Feelings
(See Workbook pages 23-28, Manual pages 96-99)

Goal: Students are asked to take a more in-depth look at their feelings.

Feelings Worksheet (page 96): This tool is designed to help students learn to verbalize their feelings in a non-threatening manner.
Identifying and Expressing Feelings (page 98): Tips to help students verbalize feelings. These are good topics for role playing.

Using Art to Express Feelings (page 99): It is best to have students do this exercise on a separate large piece of paper. Explore the following:
- The meaning and the placement of symbols.
- Which feeling is more central on the page?

- Is this what they feel most of the time or right now?
- Is this the feeling they are willing to share with the world?
- Which feelings are most intense in color?
- Which ones are close together?
- Ask them to explain their symbols

Exercise 5: The Anger Inside of Me

(See Workbook pages 29-32, Manual pages 100-102)

Goal: To discuss anger and how self-injury relates to this feeling.

Focus on the student's anger and how self-injury is often an impulsive behavior related to angry feelings. Give the student time to discuss situations when they were angry and how they handled this feeling. Encourage them to recognize their anger and explore why it is difficult for them to express it. Viewing angry feelings with sympathy and acceptance, e.g., "It's okay to get angry, everybody does"-- can help contribute to positive self-esteem and control over impulses. Also, discuss how anger affects them and their relationships. Productive ways of communicating and handling anger are processed with the counselor or group.

Optional ideas:
- Have students make a drawing/collage of what anger looks like, what makes them angry.
- Discuss fears related to anger - what has happened in the past when they were angry.
- Art option: Have students fold the long ends of a paper in toward the center so that they meet in the middle and crease them. On the outside, draw/collage anger. On the inside, draw/collage any other feelings that may be underneath the anger.

Anger Management Strategies (Workbook page 101)

Read through the strategies. Ask students which ones they are already using, which would be challenging to attempt.

Distorted Thoughts About Anger (Workbook page 102)

Ask students to complete the exercise and then discuss the answers. After discussing the answers, are there any they would want to change?

Exercise 6: Denial

(See Workbook page 33, Manual page 103)

Goal: To break through this defense mechanism to recognize that self-injury does have an impact on one's life and relationships.

There are many topics of denial that can be addressed, including: Self-injury hurts no one but me, I can stop injuring on my own, No one cares about me, etc. This can be a group discussion or debate.

Optional ideas:
· Complete self assessment worksheets.
· Read Thoughts to Challenge aloud and discuss them
· Identify different ways friends or family members have been in denial.
· Confront a peer who has been using denial statements and tell how this affects you.

Thoughts about Self-injury to Challenge

(See Workbook page 33, Manual page 103)

Common Beliefs of the Self-Injurer
From *Bodily Harm: the Breakthrough Healing Program for Self-injurers*

1. "SELF-INJURY DOESN'T HURT ANYONE."

The bottom line is that the injurers themselves are getting hurt and that their pain is important! While the physical injuries can be dangerous and even life threatening, teens don't often care about the scars; they do however care about relationships with others. Self-injury can destroy relationships, and it wounds their relationship with themselves. When someone makes the decision to injure, they are most often making a decision not to feel. In order to be in a successful relationship with others as well as oneself, one needs to be able to identify and express feelings. Thus, while the behavior does help them feel better in the short run, it is hurting them over the long haul.

2. "I DON'T UNDERSTAND WHY IT UPSETS OTHERS."

The self-injurer must learn to put her/himself in other people's shoes. Since the self-injurer is seeking empathy from others for their pain, they must be able to feel empathy for others who must confront the self-injurer all the time.

One question to ask the self-injurer is: If you had a child, would you think it was okay for your son or daughter to self-injure? If the answer is No, the follow-up question would be: Why is it an okay behavior for you, but wouldn't be good for your child?

Another challenge might be to ask if there was ever a time in her life before starting to self-injure that the concept of self-injury seemed strange to her.

3. "IT'S MY BODY AND I CAN DO WHATEVER I WANT WITH IT."

Rather than getting caught in a power struggle with the self-injurer, we prefer to acknowledge that although that may be true, we can ask the questions: "Is this truly what you want to do?" and ?Are you aware of the consequences of your behavior?"

4. "GIVING UP SELF-INJURY WILL ONLY MAKE ME HURT MORE."

At some point in the process the self-injurer may think that the treatment process is not worth the discomfort and may want to give it up. The self-injurer may want to go back to the old behavior when she comes across a feared emotion. Unfortunately, treatment may be a process where you feel worse before feeling better.

5. "THE SCARS REMIND ME OF THE BATTLE."

A question we ask the self-injurer is: What is the need to show yourself and others what you've been through, especially when a more successful alternative would be to work through the pain and move on with your life?

6. "IT'S THE BEST WAY FOR OTHERS TO SEE HOW MUCH PAIN I'M IN."

The self-injurer will often find that others will likely dismiss their emotional experience as either attention seeking or too far out of their realm for empathy, resulting in a reaction that is opposite from the one desired.

7. "NO ONE KNOWS THAT I INJURE ANYWAY."

Most self-injurers can and do keep their behavior private in the beginning, although often others may know that something is wrong. Self-injury does not occur in emotionally happy people. Sometimes others may be in denial themselves. The better the secret is kept, the more depressed the self-injurer might become.

8. "IT KEEPS PEOPLE AWAY."

Most self-injurers we've worked with fear closeness, yet simultaneously crave it. The interesting paradox is that the more you self-injure, the more likely it is that other people will intrude on your life and take control e.g., therapists and hospitals. As treatment progresses, self-injurers gradually confront this paradox.

9. "IT'S THE ONLY WAY TO KNOW IF PEOPLE REALLY CARE ABOUT ME."

Most self-injurers confuse being cared about with being taken care of. The self-injurer has a difficult time believing that other people care if they don't engage in rescue or caretaking behaviors. The rescuer ultimately feels used and severs the relationship with the self-injurer. The self-injurer doesn't see how the other person may feel overwhelmed by his/her symptoms.

10. "NEGATIVE ATTENTION IS BETTER THAN NONE."

Self-injurers often feel invisible. Getting a response from others, even if it is anger, convinces the sufferer that he/she is there and he/she is noticed.

11. "I NEED TO BE PUNISHED - I'M BAD."

Many self-injurers see themselves as fatally flawed. When asked what they've done to come to this conclusion, students are usually at a loss for words. Many believe that one or both parents don't love them, and infer that either they have done something terribly wrong or they are just unlovable. They frequently have held these beliefs for as far back as they can remember. It sometimes helps to have the self-injurer visualize an infant or young child and ask if they would label that child evil or unlovable. Almost all injurers state that children are not bad or unlovable and that even if the child is difficult, they deserve help, not punishment. This can begin the process of self-empathy and a recognition that some parents are limited in their ability to be patient and giving to their children.

12. "IT'S NOT MY FAULT - IT JUST HAPPENS."

Because self-injurers are generally unable to identify feeling states, they tend to be surprised when intense urges to injure surface. However, impulses are always connected to uncomfortable feeling states. As treatment progresses they will become more aware of the connection between feelings and impulses.

13. "I'M STRONGER THAN OTHERS. I CAN TOLERATE PAIN."

Some self-injurers are numb to the pain and may not feel anything at all when they're injuring. Pain often comes later, however, when the wounds set in or begin to heal. Some self-injurers become so numb they seek a sensation of pain to validate their existence.

14. "IF I DO NOT INJURE, I WILL DIE."

Many self-injurers have a fear that if they don't injure something terrible will happen, including their own death. In general they do not want to die, but rather want to live without the intensity of emotional pain. This is a worthy goal that, once they become able to tolerate uncomfortable feelings, is attainable without resorting to either self-injury or suicide.

Exercise 7: Emotions Surrounding Self-Injury

(See Workbook page 35, Manual page 104)

Goal: to become aware of the emotional dynamics involved in self-injurious behavior.

The ability to identify their feelings or thoughts that lead up to an episode of self-harm can help them conquer the behavior by placing its origin in the proper context. This type of self awareness will help them to begin thinking and analyzing themselves and their motives before taking action against their bodies.

Exercise 8: Nurturing Myself

(See Workbook page 37, Manual page 105)

Goal: to develop self-soothing behavior to redirect one from self-injury and promote self-esteem.

Saying goodbye to self-injury will bring up many feelings for self-injurers. In order to do this safely, it is important for them to be able to nurture themselves. It is not unusual for self-injurers to need to put nurturing time on their calendars and to do so until it becomes a welcome desire.

Many people have trouble nurturing themselves because they don't believe they deserve it. Thus, they have often failed to develop strategies to consciously alleviate any discomfort. It is important for them to understand that taking care of oneself is not selfish, but rather selfless. Each of us has an obligation to take care of ourselves so that we can remain healthy and happy. Flight attendants instruct us that in the event of an emergency, adults are to put the oxygen mask on themselves before their children. In other words, it is impossible for us to care for others if we don't take care of ourselves.

1. Ask students to nurture themselves at least once a day.

2. Have them record the way in which they nurtured themselves and how they felt. For example: taking a bubble bath, going out to dinner or a show, getting a massage, etc.

Exercise 9: Creative Writing

(See Workbook page 39, Manual page 106)

Goal: To give students an opportunity to share works written by themselves or others that were used to express feelings or thoughts.

Students present excerpts of creative expression, originating from self or others. It can be a poem, a short story, an affirmation, a greeting card, a Bible passage or anything which sparks creativity. They are asked to explain how this excerpt is relevant to their own life. This often leads to discussion of therapeutic issues, which can be beneficial. If shared in a group setting, each person should be given an opportunity to check-in.

Optional ideas: Have them write their thoughts on expectations (i.e., society, parents, and their own); write their thoughts on recovery or self-injury.

Exercise 10: Saying Goodbye to Self-injury
(See Workbook page 41, Manual page 107)

Goal: To allow students to acknowledge that self-injury has played an important role in their lives and will represent a loss, while at the same time recognizing that self-injury had kept them from experiencing their full range of feelings. The goal is that by saying good-bye to self-injury they are stating that they are no longer afraid of feeling.

Exercise 11: The Person I Want to Be
(See Workbook page 43, Manual page 108)

Goal: to identify positive goals and personality characteristics that students want to enhance.

Setting goals for giving up self-injury involves adding new thoughts, behaviors, interests and gratifications to replace the old symptoms.

Now it's time to begin to look ahead to finding enjoyment and success for themselves. Were there activities they enjoyed when they were younger (e.g., making new friends or enjoying certain classes) that they would like to try again? If not, then maybe there are things they have heard about or seen on T.V. that look like fun or would be rewarding. Encourage them to dream big! Remind them to not limit themselves with negative thinking.

Section V

WORKBOOK EXERCISES

Exercise 1

(See Workbook pages 7-10, Manual page 69)

Process Questions and Alternatives

Self-injury is an impulsive act. Answering these questions will give you an opportunity to think about the incident and the response you chose to make.

Self injury is a way of displacing feelings from the head to the body. You may have trouble identifying feelings. A feeling list is provided to help you identify what you are feeling. Feelings are valuable clues to what needs to be looked at, worked through and resolved. The ability to sit with feelings and not be overwhelmed is a strong sign of recovery.

To help understand what happened or has been happening, please answer the following questions:

What did you...

Think?_____

_____

_____

_____

_____

_____

Feel?_____

_____

_____

_____

_____

_____

Believe? _____

_____

_____

_____

_____

_____

Want? _____

_____

_____

_____

_____

_____

Need? _____

_____

_____

_____

_____

_____

Choose? _____

_____

_____

_____

_____

_____

Until you are able to manage your impulses, it is very important to have support from people you trust. Please look at the Keeping Myself Safe form on page 49, fill it out and sign it in the presence of someone you trust.

Need Help Identifying Feelings?

MAD

Annoyed

Furious

Enraged

Angry

Ticked Off

Irritated

Frustrated

Livid

Aggravated

GLAD

Blissful

Proud

Ecstatic

Curious

Loving

Cheerful

Relaxed

Relieved

Happy

ANXIOUS

Vulnerable

Excited

Startled

Frightened

Terrified

Agitated

Shocked

Surprised

Scared

SAD

Depressed

Agonized

Exhausted

Tired

Grieving

Hurt

Lonely

Miserable

Empty

My S.A.F.E. Alternatives (Workbook page 10)

Alternatives: These are temporary distractions when impulses are very strong and you need to get some emotional distance before you can process the impulse.

Begin to list your Alternatives to use when you have the urge to injure.
When you have an impulse to injure, you may be overwhelmed and unable to think of healthy options. You may not be able to think of 18 right away, so continue to add to the list as you discover other activities you find helpful,

1.

2.

3.

4.

5.

6.

7.

8.

9.

10.

11.

12.

13.

14.

15.

16.

17.

18.

Exercise 2

(See Workbook pages11 - 20 and Manual page 69)

Learning to Use Logs

Impulse Control Log® The Impulse Control Log® was designed to help you think through your impulses before you choose to act on them. It helps you to focus on the reason *behind* the impulse to injure, rather than focusing on the impulse itself. Begin to recognize patterns behind the impulses such as time of day, location where the impulses occur, and precipitating events (e.g., conflict with a parent or significant other, illness or death of a friend, etc.).

It is important that you be specific on the log as global responses are not generally helpful. An example of a global entry would be *"A teacher made me very angry."* A better entry would be *"A teacher said that I talked too much and it made me mad."*

S.A.F.E. ALTERNATIVES® Impulse Control Log® - Side 1

ACTING OUT/SELF INJURY THOUGHTS: (e.g., cutting, running away)	TIME AND DATE: (e.g., 9:00 P.M. 2/15/0?)	LOCATION: (e.g., bedroom)	SITUATION: (e.g., I was by myself, thinking about getting better.)	FEELING: (e.g., scared)	WHAT WOULD BE THE RESULT OF SELF-INJURY? (e.g., more scars, loss of trust of family / friends)

S.A.F.E. ALTERNATIVES® Impulse Control Log® – Side 2

WHAT WOULD I BE TRYING TO COMMUNICATE WITH MY SELF-INJURY? (e.g., I'm scared and I need attention.)	ACTION TAKEN: How were thoughts/feelings communicated or coped with? (e.g., I used my five alternatives and confronted my distorted thoughts.)	OUTCOME: (e.g., I noticed a decrease in my desire to act out.)

More Logs:

(See Workbook page 14, Manual page 70)

Once you have learned to use the Impulse Control Log® you might want
to utilize one of the following more specific logs.

1. Confrontation Log®: This log is designed to help you think through and
manage confrontation. Confrontation is not pleasant for most of us, but for self-
injurers, who often harbor tremendous fears of abandonment, confrontation can
become particularly difficult. Since it is so difficult, people often respond in
extremes: either avoiding confrontation all together; or confronting in a hostile,
aggressive manner. The goal is to challenge irrational thoughts so that you are
better able to assert needs in an appropriate manner.

2. Dilemma Log®: This log is designed to help you think through dilemmas,
challenging irrational/catastrophic thinking to come up with a healthy solution.

> Examples: *You are aware that a peer has self-injured. Do you tell,
> or do you keep the secret?*
>
> *You see another student cheating, do you tell?*
>
> *Your best friend's boyfriend is cheating on her. Do you
> let her know?*

This log helps one to think through the consequences of each decision.

3. Productive Risk Taking Log®: This log was designed to help you plan an
action or verbally communicate a need or concern that is out of your comfort
zone. People would rather tolerate their own misery than take a risk to change.
Dwelling on a failed outcome can often paralyze you from taking a risk. This log
helps you carefully plan strategies for moving on in your life.

- Preparing to take a risk is the first step.
  Example: *The risk may be to share something personal and painful.
  The fear is that your peers will think "badly" of you.*

- Next, decide how you want to proceed with the risk and when.
  Example: *You want to take this risk in group.*

- Identify what you hope to accomplish by taking this risk.
  Example: *That you may became closer to the group, that other
  peers will share similar experiences and that, regardless
  of the outcome, you need to share as a way to heal.*

- Record the outcome of the risk taken.

Example: *You may say it was not as bad as you thought it would be or that you were surprised at how others opened up because you opened up.*

· The last entry tells what you learned about yourself by taking this risk.

Example: *You may learn that you do not have to be alone in your pain, and that you have strengths, and most importantly, that you can expand your comfort zone with each risk.*

4. **Negative Thinking Log**®: This log was designed to help you organize how you think about yourself and challenge your belief system. Most people do not realize just how often negative thinking leads to self-injurious behavior. When asked to explore their thoughts, most self-injurers say they do not know how to think in ways that are not negative. This log guides you into thinking differently. Use these three steps when a negative thought arises.

· The first step is to write down the negative Question/Statement.

Example: *"Why do I think of myself as "bad"? Or "I am stupid" or "I need to be punished" etc...?*

· The next step is to write down the Belief.

Example: *"I think I"m "bad" because I caused my parents to divorce".*

· The last step is to Challenge these statements and beliefs.

Example: *"Maybe my parents just could not get along, and their divorce had nothing to do with me."*

It will take time to become comfortable "logging", **and** it is worth the effort.

S.A.F.E. ALTERNATIVES®
Self Abuse Finally Ends

Confrontation Log®

(See Workbook page 16, Manual page 70)
Learning to Confront Effectively

What is a confrontation? A confrontation is the act of stating one's opinion in order to bring about change, or the act of challenging one's own negative thinking.

> Example 1: *Telling another person that you experienced their behavior or comment as destructive/abusive.*

> Example 2: *Challenge means to call into question as to why you think you are "bad", "stupid", "need to be punished", etc...*

Whom are you confronting and why? _____

_____

How do you plan to confront this person(s) and when? _____

_____

What do you hope to accomplish by confronting this person(s)?_____

_____

_____

Outcome of confrontation _____

_____

What did you learn about yourself from this confrontation?_____

_____

Negative thoughts about yourself _____

_____

What questions or challenges did you ask of yourself?_____

_____

What did you learn about yourself from this challenge? _____

_____

_____

S.A.F.E. ALTERNATIVES®
Self Abuse Finally Ends

Dilemma Log®(See Workbook page 17, Manual page 70)

What is a dilemma? A dilemma is an undesirable or unpleasant conflict.

> Example: *A friend just told you something that could cause harm and asked you to not tell anyone.*

Write down your dilemma. _____

_____

_____

Write down your thoughts regarding your dilemma. _____

_____

_____

How are you dealing with your dilemma? _____

_____

_____

Have you shared your dilemma with anyone? Yes___ No___

   If yes, with whom? _____

   If no, why not? _____

Have you decided on an outcome scenario for your dilemma? Yes___ No___

   If yes, is this outcome realistic? Yes___ No___

Do you find yourself ruminating over this outcome? Yes___ No___ NA___

Outcome:_____

_____

_____

What steps will you take when a dilemma arises? _____

_____

_____

What have you learned about how you deal with dilemmas? _____

_____

S.A.F.E. ALTERNATIVES®
Self Abuse Finally Ends

Productive Risk Taking Log®

(See Workbook page 18, Manual page 71)

Productive risk taking is acting on or verbally communicating a need or a concern which is out of one's comfort zone.

> Example: *Setting a limit, or saying "no" to a friend.*

Describe the risk. _____

_____

_____

Write your fear(s) about this risk: _____

_____

_____

How do you plan to take this risk and when? _____

_____

_____

What do you hope to accomplish by taking this risk? _____

_____

_____

OUTCOME:

Describe how the risk turned out. _____

_____

_____

What did you learn about yourself by taking this risk? _____

_____

_____

_____

S.A.F.E. ALTERNATIVES®
Self Abuse Finally Ends

Negative Thinking Log®

(See Workbook page 19, Manual page 71)

Challenging negative thinking means to call into question one's own beliefs or thoughts.

Example:

Question/Statement: *Why do I think of myself as "bad"? Or "I am stupid" or "I need to be punished", etc...*

Belief: *I think I am bad because I caused my parents to divorce.*

Challenge: *Maybe my parents just could not get along, and their divorce had nothing to do with me.*

Question/Statement: _____

Belief: _____

Challenge: _____

Question/Statement: _____

Belief: _____

Challenge: _____

Question/Statement: _____

Belief: _____

Challenge: _____

Question/Statement: _____

Belief: _____

Challenge: _____

Exercise 3

(See Workbook page 21, Manual page 72)

How Do I See Myself?

A) What am I like as a person? (i.e., emotionally, intellectually, in manner and behavior)

B) What are my roles, and how do I think and feel about them? (i.e., as a female/male, teenager, student, daughter/son, sister/brother or employee)

C) What are my particular strengths (use the following page to help you) and weaknesses as a person? What do I need/want to change? What traits would I never change?

A List of MY Positive Qualities

(See Workbook page 22)

Positive things I know about myself or have heard from others.

I AM _____

I AM _____

I AM _____

I AM _____

I AM _____

I AM _____

I AM _____

I AM _____

I AM _____

I AM _____

I AM _____

I AM _____

I AM _____

I AM _____

I AM _____

I AM _____

I AM _____

I AM _____

I AM _____

I AM _____

I AM _____

Exercise 4

(See Workbook page 23, Manual page 72)

Talking About Feelings

1. Are you usually aware of your feelings?

2. What clues do you have to what you are feeling?

3. Who do you usually share your feelings with?

4. Do you ever cover what you are feeling with another feeling? If so, what feeling do you cover and what feeling do you express?

5. How are feelings expressed in your family?

6. How do you know when you are feeling angry?

7. How do you express your anger?

8. With whom do you share your angry feelings?

9. Do you ever cover your anger with other feelings?

10. Do others share their angry feelings with you? If so, who?

11. How do you react to others when they are angry?

12. Whose feelings are more important, yours or others?

13. Have you ever been depressed and not known why?

14. What do you do if you are feeling depressed?

15. Do you label your feelings of depression with other feelings?

16. Who do you share your feelings of depression with?

17. If you are feeling depressed, do you recognize why?

18. Do you often feel anxious?

19. What type of situation brings on your anxiety?

20. Are you able to identify your thoughts when you are anxious? What are they?

21. If you are anxious, how do you cope with this feeling?

22. Who do you share your anxiety with?

23. When do you experience happy feelings? Who do you share them with?

24. What have you learned about yourself and your feelings from this questionnaire?

Identifying and Expressing Feelings

(See Workbook page 25, Manual page 72)

The next time that you are in a situation that stirs up strong emotions, use the tips below to help you express yourself.

1. Stop and think *"What am I feeling? What is causing the feeling? Who is involved?"*

2. Ask yourself, *"Who can I talk to about these feelings?"* If you feel angry or hurt by someone, consider letting that person know why.

3. Give yourself time to calm down and then find the earliest opportunity to talk privately with the person. Waiting too long can lower your willingness to communicate.

4. Express your feelings as honestly and respectfully as you can, using "I" statements. e.g., *"When I hear you raise your voice, I am scared because….."*

5. It is okay to be angry, but it is not necessary to yell, call names or accuse the other person.

6. Be prepared to discuss your feelings.

7. Give the other person a chance to respond or explain. Be attentive to their feedback.

8. If you need something from the other person, make that need clear. For example, if your sister plays loud music while you are studying, ask her to think about your feelings and turn the music down.

9. If the person does not respect what you are saying or will not listen, accept it. You cannot change other people or decide how they will act. You can only tell them how you feel and think.

10. Find someone else to talk with — a teacher, friend, school counselor or relative. There is always someone who will listen. If the first person won't listen, try another until you find someone who will.

Using Art to Express Feelings
(See Workbook page 27, Manual page 72)

Use a Color/Symbol to Represent These Feelings
(Label the emotions)

Vulnerable

Scared

Loved

Frustrated

Depressed

Hurt

Happy

Angry

_____ (you choose)

Exercise 5

(See Workbook page 29, Manual page 73)

The Anger Inside of Me

A) What does becoming angry feel like?

B) What kinds of thoughts arise once I'm aware that I'm angry?

C) Am I afraid of others seeing my anger? Why?

D) What do I need to learn about handling my anger?

S.A.F.E. ALTERNATIVES®
Self Abuse Finally Ends

Anger Management Strategies
(See Workbook page 31, Manual page 73)

- Be aware of your anger. It is your body's signal that something is wrong.

- Take time out to identify the feelings that may have preceded your anger.

- Remember that anger is a natural human emotion, not an action.

- Remember that it is alright to feel anger. Being angry and expressing that anger are separate issues. Rage and violence are inappropriate ways to express anger.

- It is helpful to remember these facts about anger:
Anger originates within the angry person.
Feelings come from thoughts.
I think my own thoughts.
Thoughts are based on beliefs.
Anger is usually preceded by anxiety, fear, or hurt.

- Be aware of distorted appraisals or unrealistic thoughts that lead to anger. Challenge distorted thoughts about anger and replace them with more realistic thoughts about anger.

- Relaxation exercises can be used to help one gain control over the body's reactions to anger. When you are able to maintain increased control over your body's reactions to anger, you increase your capacity to be self-soothing and are able to think more clearly.

S.A.F.E. ALTERNATIVES®
Self Abuse Finally Ends

Distorted Thoughts about Anger
(See Workbook page 32, Manual page 73)

Take 10 minutes to complete the exercise, and then share your answers with the group or your counselor.

	Never	Sometimes	Frequently	Always
1. I must never feel angry.	____	____	____	____
2. I am a bad person if I feel angry.	____	____	____	____
3. People will not love me if I express anger.	____	____	____	____
4. People will reject me if I express anger.	____	____	____	____
5. If I'm angry I must be out of control.	____	____	____	____
6. People should know I'm angr without my having to tell them.	____	____	____	____
7. If I'm angry, people should do things to make me feel less angry	____	____	____	____
8. People will like me better if I never express anger.	____	____	____	____
9. I must never show anger toward my family.	____	____	____	____
10. If I become angry, I might stay angry forever	____	____	____	____
11. I must be right about an issue before I can be angry.	____	____	____	____
12. I need to have logical reasons, before I can be angry.	____	____	____	____

Exercise 6

(See Workbook page 33, Manual pages 74-76)

Denial: a defense mechanism that reinforces the belief that self-injury does *not* have an impact on one's life and relationships. See if you can challenge these common beliefs held by self-injurers.

Thoughts about self-injury to challenge

- Self-injury doesn't hurt anyone

- It shouldn't upset others

- It's my body; I can do whatever I want

- Giving up self-injury will hurt worse

- The scars remind me of the battle

- It is okay because no one knows I injure

- It's the only way to know that people care

- Negative attention is better than no attention

- It keeps people away

- I need to be punished, I am a bad person

- I can't control it

- If I don't self-injure I won't have anything, so I will have to kill myself

- It's the only thing that works

- It's an addiction

- I only do it in private

- I can stop anytime

- No one understands

- It's not a problem

- Add your own......

Exercise 7

(See Workbook page 35, Manual page 77)

Emotions Surrounding Self-Injury

A) What feelings/thoughts do I typically have prior to, during and after an episode of self-injury?

B) What feelings have I wanted to create in others through self-injurious behavior?

C) What feelings/reactions do I bring out in others, even if not intended?

Exercise 8

(See Workbook page 37, Manual page 77)

Nurturing Myself

This assignment will help you develop self-soothing behavior, which can divert you from self-injury and promote self esteem.

A) List 25 ways I can take care of myself and give myself a lift - special ways to experience being content.

B) What, if anything, keeps me from nurturing myself more often?

Exercise 9

(See workbook page 39, Manual page 77)

Creative Writing

This is an opportunity to share works that you have written or read that helped express your feelings or thoughts. (Please do not use anything graphic or that has caused you to injure.)

A) Give an excerpt of creative expression originating from yourself or others. It can be a poem, a short story, an affirmation, a greeting card, a Bible passage or anything which has meaning to you. Explain how this excerpt is relevant to your life.

B) Write your thoughts on expectations (i.e., society, parents, and your own).

C) Write your thoughts on recovery or self-injury.

Exercise 10

(See Workbook page 41, Manual page 78)

Saying Goodbye to Self-injury

A) How do I imagine my life will be without self-injurious behavior?

B) What will I miss about my "old" ways?

C) What new definition do I want to apply to myself now?

D) Write a letter saying goodbye to self-injury. Describe how you said goodbye. Include all thoughts and feelings related to this assignment.

Exercise 11

(See Workbook page 43, Manual page 78)

The Person I Want to Be

A) How do I want my life to be?

B) Identify attitudes, beliefs, feelings and behaviors that interfere with making progress towards this goal.

C) What am I willing to change to accomplish my goals?

S.A.F.E. ALTERNATIVES®
Self Abuse Finally Ends

Group Expectations
(See Workbook page 45)

(Guidelines to be used in a group setting; they are also very effective in the classroom.)

· Use "I" statements

· Allow one person to talk at a time

· Be respectful of self, peers and staff

· Be attentive – sit up, no side conversations or sleeping

· Offer constructive feedback

· Maintain appropriate boundaries at all times

· Talk about the action, not the person

· Challenge a peer who is reluctant to do something new or different

· No writing during group

· No eating during group

· No profanity or graphic language

S.A.F.E. ALTERNATIVES®
Self Abuse Finally Ends

Tips to Help You Get the Most Out of Group
(Workbook page 46)

- Learn how to use the Impulse Control Log® as soon as possible. If you are confused about what you ought to be logging, discuss your questions/thoughts with the counselor and/or your peers.
- Give feedback; state what you see or hear and how it relates to you.
- Take time (focus on the issues you need to work on); don't waste your time.
- Participate as fully as possible. The more you put in, the more you'll take out.
- Use "I" statements.
- Keep an open mind. Be willing to discover positive, negative, growing and limiting sides of yourself.
- See the group as a safe place for growth. Group is a place for progress, not perfection.
- Use the group to practice new behaviors.
- Think of ways to apply what you are learning in group to your life in and out of group.
- Pay attention to your own body language and feelings. Don't shut them out.
- Avoid postponing the risk-taking involved in letting others know you. Keep in mind that you will really have a better chance to grow with the help of your peers.
- You earned your seat in group. Don't apologize for your statements.
- Be considerate, helpful, open and trusting. Allow yourself to take risks.
- Be noise-considerate (no shuffling papers).
- Remember: Change takes time and effort.

S.A.F.E. ALTERNATIVES®
Self Abuse Finally Ends

Strategies for Communicating Safely With Others
(Workbook page 47)

- Listen attentively.

- Express your feelings honestly.

- Speak to people directly.

- Speak in the first person ("I"), and only speak for yourself.

- Work diligently to always be aware of your own thoughts and feelings.

- Learn to read your own and other's body language.

- Be spontaneous.

- Be aware of your behavior and the roles you play with peers and staff.

- Work to have genuine encounters with others.

- Be patient and comfortable with silence.

- Recognize that trust is not something that just happens – you play a crucial role in creating it.

- If you are aware of anything getting in the way of a climate of safety, share your hesitations with the group.

- Commit to getting the most from each group by focusing on your goals.

- Realize that if the work your peers are doing is affecting you, it is crucial that you let them know how you're reacting. If you are able to identify with the struggles or pains of others, it helps everyone if you share your thoughts and feelings.

- Decide for yourself (and/or with guidance from your therapist) what, how much and when you will disclose personal stories. Others will not have a basis of knowing you unless you openly tell them about yourself.

- If you are having trouble sharing yourself personally, it may help to begin by letting your peers know what makes it hard for you to talk about yourself.

- Be respectful to all in language and action.

S.A.F.E. ALTERNATIVES
Self Abuse Finally Ends

Strategies for Giving Feedback
(Workbook page 48)

In group, you can work on your communication skills and reflect on your issues while peers discuss their issues. You will learn to give appropriate, constructive feedback to peers. When you begin to share your stories, you will also receive valuable feedback. Use the following strategies when giving feedback:

§   Ask permission

§   Use good timing

§   Have a positive attitude

§   Use "I" statements

§   Talk about the action, not the person

§   Offer alternatives/suggestions

§   Use simple, DIRECT statements

§   Use respectful language

§   Challenge a peer who is reluctant to do something new and/or difficult

§   Remind peers to use their logs, (e.g., "log it")

§   Share how the discussion relates to your issues/feelings

S.A.F.E. ALTERNATIVES® Programs

S.A.F.E. Intensive® is a 30-day intensive treatment program for persons 13 and over who engage in repeated self-injurious behavior. The multidisciplinary treatment team uses various therapies to support and empower individuals to make healthy choices in dealing with emotional distress. The treatment program is approximately 30 days of programming. The program is voluntary, and therefore, patients must be motivated to stop self-destructive behaviors. On admission, the patient signs a safety contract agreeing to refrain from any self-injurious behaviors for the entire length of treatment. Patients will be asked to address all forms of self-injury, including food and nutrition issues. In addition, patients are expected to identify and use alternatives to self-injury provided by the program.

S.A.F.E. Expressions® are partial hospitalization programs (PHP) for adults and adolescents whose self-injurious behavior negatively impacts their lives. Those individuals who do not require inpatient hospitalization and whose safety can be maintained on an outpatient basis are appropriate candidates. Because adolescents, and some adults, are ambivalent about giving up self-injury, treatment continues even if the person is not motivated to stop the injuring. Everyone participating in S.A.F.E. Expressions® will be asked to sign a S.A.F.E. Promise upon admission, stating that they will attempt to refrain from self-destructive behaviors by using alternatives they learn in the program.

S.A.F.E. Choice® is a group psychotherapy program that is offered in six-week segments. Appropriate candidates are adolescents and adults who self-injure and want to change the behavior. Participants may have attended one of the S.A.F.E. ALTERNATIVES® Programs, but it is not a requirement. Group size will be limited to 10-12 members. Groups are offered for adults and adolescents, and each is facilitated by a licensed clinical therapist. Prospective members are expected to be in individual or family outpatient therapy.

S.A.F.E. Focus® is a voluntary support group which utilizes guidelines developed by the S.A.F.E. ALTERNATIVES® Program. You can facilitate a group in your area. This support group focuses on identifying, verbalizing and tolerating feelings, rather than on underlying issues. As participants begin to engage in this work, they may recognize similar, if not identical, behaviors in fellow group members. Such recognition may be uncomfortable, yet it is highly beneficial because awareness is the first step towards recovery. Additional emphasis is placed on group interaction by using verbal communication and developing interpersonal skills. Participants will learn to take in and give constructive feedback. The importance of healthy risk-taking will be stressed in order to provide the participant with an opportunity to develop new coping skills in place of self-injury. We strongly recommend that each group member be simultaneously engaged in individual therapy for the duration of the group sessions. S.A.F.E. Focus® is not a replacement for one on one psychotherapy, it is a support group.

For a current listing of our programs and services, please visit selfinjury.com.

About Our Founders

Karen Conterio, CEO of S.A.F.E. ALTERNATIVES®

Karen Conterio is the CEO of the S.A.F.E. ALTERNATIVES® Program. The program was founded by Karen Conterio in 1985 as the first outpatient support group for those who engage in repetitive self harm behavior. Then, in 1986, Ms. Conterio teamed with Wendy Lader, Ph.D. to offer the first structured inpatient program for deliberate self harm behavior.

Ms. Conterio was trained and certified as an alcohol and addictions counselor and is also a certified group facilitator. She is the co-author, with Wendy Lader, of the book *Bodily Harm: the Breakthrough Healing Program for Self-Injurers* (Hyperion, 1998) which outlines the S.A.F.E. ALTERNATIVES® philosophy and treatment protocol. Ms. Conterio co-authored research on self-mutilation published in Community Mental Health Journal, ActaPsychiatric Scandinavia, and Suicide and Life Threatening Behavior.

She has given in-services and lectures since 1987 and has done hundreds of radio, magazine and newspaper interviews, including Time, Newsweek, the Sun Times, the Chicago Tribune, Forbes, the St. Louis Post-Dispatch, Nursing Spectrum, Cincinnati Enquirer, World Talk Radio and Ann Landers (who has frequently recommended the S.A.F.E. ALTERNATIVES® Program and 800 - DONTCUT® information line in her column). Ms. Conterio has appeared on numerous television shows since 1987 including: CNN; Dateline NBC; Good Morning America; Oprah Winfrey; Phil Donahue; Larry King Live; Women's Entertainment Network-Secret Lives of Women; CBS-2 Chicago and ABC World News Tonight. She was a featured expert on self-injury in the following magazines: Allure; Seventeen; Sassy and New York Times Sunday Magazine. Internationally, both Ms. Conterio and Dr. Lader were interviewed for CAPA (French television), Catholic University of Chile TV Network Corporation and Univision for multiple network programs, Telemundo, and Marie Claire (French). Lastly, Ms. Conterio has served as a consultant for several television and movie scripts including the television series 90210, 7th Heaven, CUT, Channel One News and two Lifetime productions (Odd Girl Out and Painful Secrets).

Wendy Lader, Ph.D., M.Ed., President & Clinical Director of S.A.F.E. ALTERNATIVES®

Dr. Lader, an expert in women's issues, teamed with Karen Conterio in 1986 to offer the first structured inpatient program for deliberate self-harm behavior. Dr. Lader was the Director of the Girls Program at Mercy Hospital and Medical Center, and the Women's Program at Hartgrove Hospital in Chicago. She also served as a clinical consultant to the Women's Services program at the Metro YWCA in Chicago (1991–2004) as well as a member on the Illinois State's Attorney's Task Force on Women's Issues (1985-1989).

Dr. Lader earned her Ph.D. degree in Clinical Psychology and her M.Ed. in Special Education. She is an international speaker on self-injury, and highly regarded as an expert in the field. Her workshops and seminars draw hundreds of professionals. Dr. Lader is cited and published in multiple professional journals including: Journal of Clinical Psychology/In Session; Psychiatry Research; Psychological Reports; Counselor; Paradigm; Advance for Nurse Practitioners; Counseling Today; Medlife; Ask Dr. Drew; the Brown University Child/Adolescent Behavior Letter and the Medical Tribune. She has been featured in several medical productions including: Web MD; American Psychological Association; Associated Press and CBS News Health Watch. She is the co-author, with Ms. Conterio, of the book, *Bodily Harm: the Breakthrough Healing Program for Self-Injurers* (Hyperion, 1998). Dr. Lader is a founding member of ISSS (The International Society for the Study of Self-Injury).

In addition, Dr. Lader has appeared on TV shows such as **The Dr Drew Show,** The Today Show, Dateline, NBC, Good Morning America, The Oprah Winfrey Show, CNN, 20/20, Geraldo, The Morning Show, The Shirley Show (Canada), Lifestyle Magazine, Regis, ABC World News,The Tonight, and A&E Interventions. She has been quoted in numerous print articles, e.g., New York Times Magazine, Time, Newsweek, Teen Vogue, Teen People, Cosmo Girl, Today's Christian Woman, Christian Parenting Today, Ask Amy, Seventeen, and Reader's Digest.

CEUs NOW AVAILABLE

The founders of the first short-term self-injury treatment program in the country offer groundbreaking help for a dangerous and increasingly widespread syndrome

Bodily Harm

THE BREAKTHROUGH

HEALING PROGRAM

FOR SELF-INJURERS

Karen Conterio and Wendy Lader, Ph.D.
with Jennifer Kingson Bloom

Bodily Harm is an authoritative examination of the behavior of self-injury. It is the first to offer a comprehensive treatment regimen. Written by the founders of S.A.F.E. ALTERNATIVES© (Self Abuse Finally Ends), it clearly defines self-injury and explains the kind of emotional trauma that can lead to self-injurious behaviors. It includes case studies, diaries, and success stories from a diverse group of patients. Most importantly, Bodily Harm offers a course of treatment based on years of experience and extensive clinical research – as well as compassion, advice, and hope for the afflicted and their loved ones.

National Association of Social Workers (NASW) and National Board of Certified Counselors (NBCC) have approved this home study course for 10 CEUs towards the following licenses: LSW/LCSW and LPC/LCPC. After reading Bodily Harm, you may purchase the home-study exam at www.selfinjury.com. Upon passing the exam, you will be issued a certificate for 10 CEUs. S.A.F. E. ALTERNATIVES® is an NBCC-Approved Continuing Education Provider (ACEP) and may offer NBCC-approved clock hours for events that meet NBCC requirements. The ACEP solely is responsible for all aspects of the program.

RESOURCES

◻ *Self-Injury: A Manual For School Professionals*

SCHOOL PROFESSIONALS WILL LEARN:

To identify the various forms and purposes of self-injury, the DO'S and DON'TS for counselors, nurses and teachers, how to assess for self-injury and suicide, specific intervention techniques and tools, how to talk to parents about self-injury, to identify resources and referrals for self-injurers who are in need of services outside of school, how to create a smooth transition for students returning to school from hospitalization or other forms of intensive treatment, and so much more.......

◻ *Student Workbook* - designed to accompany *Self-Injury: A Manual for School Professionals*. (above)

This Workbook can be used as an individual intervention (e.g., given to a student to complete on their own and then review with a staff member) or as a format for a more in-depth individual session with a counselor or in a group setting. The exercises can be used randomly or in order. It is possible to "pick and choose" the parts of exercises that are relevant at a given time.

◻ *Beyond the Razor's Edge* *A Journey of Healing and Hope Beyond Self-Injury*, by Judy Redheffer and Sarah Brecht. This book is filled with stories of self-injurers' journeys from self-loathing to self-love; from histories of pain to futures of contentment. It describes how people seeking physical pain in an effort to soothe their intense emotional pain learned to face and embrace their full range of emotions leading them to happier and more fulfilling lives.

◻ "Can You See My Pain"- DVD includes personnel stories as well as expert testimonials and comments by Karen Conterio and Wendy Lader, Ph.D., founders of S.A.F.E. ALTERNATIVES®. Through first-hand accounts, this program gives self-injurers a chance to tell their stories and talk about what they are doing to stop self-injuring themselves. These poignant stories are punctuated by comments from clinicians from S.A.F.E. ALTERNATIVES®, the first in-patient program in the country specifically designed to help self-injurers. An excellent resource for self-injurers, families, private practitioners, schools, and healthcare providers. Running time: 30 minutes.

S.A.F.E. Focus® Leader Manual

S.A.F.E. Focus® is a voluntary support group which utilizes guidelines developed by the S.A.F.E. ALTERNATIVES® Program. This support group focuses on identifying, verbalizing, and tolerating feelings, rather than on underlying issues. Please visit our website to view the table of contents for this manual.

S.A.F.E. Focus® Participant Manual

Would you like to start or join a self help group for Self Injury?
S.A.F.E. Focus® is a voluntary support group which utilizes guidelines developed by the S.A.F.E. ALTERNATIVES® Program. This support group focuses on identifying, verbalizing, and tolerating feelings, rather than on underlying issues.

CUT - Teens and Self-Injury DVD

Award Winning Documentary featuring Karen Conterio. Provides an intimate look at a largely unacknowledged problem that affects thousands of young people, their families and friends. Using the words, music and artwork of the teens themselves, director Wendy Schneider draws back the curtain on the secrecy surrounding the cycle of self-harm and brings this hidden issue into sharp, clear focus. Compelling, incisive and profoundly moving, CUT issues a call to bring the problem of self-injury out of the shadows and reminds us that the first step towards healing is an honest acknowledgment of reality. Includes music by Garbage, Plumb, Gina Young, and Cyndi Boste. Running Time: 57 minutes.

Please visit the store at selfinjury.com for a current list of prices.

S.A.F.E. ALTERNATIVES®
Self Abuse Finally Ends

WAYS TO GET AND STAY CONNECTED TO S.A.F.E. ALTERNATIVES®

Join us on the blog at www.selfinjury.com/blog. Our blog is a safe place to go on-line for trigger free support. It's a place for people who self injure and/or their loved ones to reach out for support and advice.

Read more about our program in the book *Bodily Harm* written by S.A.F.E. co-founders Karen Conterio and Dr. Wendy Lader. Pass along the information to those who are also in recovery from self-injury.

Download the S.A.F.E. ALTERNATIVES® app – have privacy secured logs on hand at all times.

"Like" us on Facebook at   S.A.F.E. (Self Abuse Finally Ends) ALTERNATIVES®